Introduction

> *A second issue involves the effect of the large volume of reserves created as we buy assets. [. . .] The huge quantity of bank reserves that were created has been seen largely as a byproduct of the purchases that would be unlikely to have a significant independent effect on financial markets and the economy. This view is not consistent with the simple models in many textbooks or the monetarist tradition in monetary policy, which emphasizes a line of causation from reserves to the money supply to economic activity and inflation. . . . [W]e will need to watch and study this channel carefully.*
> *Donald L. Kohn, Vice Chairman of the Federal Reserve Board, March 24, 2010*

The Federal Reserve's implementation of a range of nontraditional monetary policy measures to combat a severe financial crisis and a deep economic recession resulted in a very large increase in the level of reserve balances in the U.S. banking system. As a result, there has been renewed interest in the transmission of monetary policy from reserves to the rest of the economy. Since the 1980s, two broad transmission mechanisms have been discussed: an "interest-rate" or "money channel," in which interest rates adjust to clear markets and influence borrowing and lending behavior; and a "credit channel," in which the quantity as much as the price of loanable funds transmit monetary policy to the economy. Within the credit channel literature, a narrow "bank lending channel" view of the world follows the textbook money multiplier taught in undergraduate textbooks and suggests that changes in open market operations and the quantity of reserves directly affect the amount of lending that banks can do.

A textbook money multiplier and the bank lending channel imply an important role for money in the transmission mechanism. In the past couple of decades however, New Keynesian models used for macroeconomic policy analysis have excluded money. The exceptions in this class of models are those where a money demand equation is appended, and the quantity of money is entirely endogenously determined with no feedback to real variables. This extreme marginalization of money is not universal, however. Some researchers for example, Hafer, Haslag, and Jones (2007), Leeper and Roush (2003), Ireland (2004), Meltzer (2001) and most notably, the European Central Bank, put serious weight on the role of money in the macroeconomy and policy analysis. Indeed, at the other extreme, many economics textbooks and some academic research, such as Freeman and Kydland (2000) or Diamond and Rajan (2006) continue to refer to the very narrow money multiplier and accord it a principle role in the transmission of monetary policy.

The recent rise in reserve balances suggests a need to reassess the link from reserves to money and to bank lending. We argue that the institutional structure in the United States and empirical evidence based on data since 1990 both strongly suggest that the transmission mechanism does not work through the standard money multiplier model from reserves to money and bank loans. In the absence of a multiplier, open market operations, which simply change reserve balances, do not directly affect lending behavior at the aggregate level.[1] Put differently, if the quantity of reserves is relevant for the transmission of monetary policy, a different mechanism must be found. The argument against the textbook money multiplier is not new. For example, Bernanke and Blinder (1988) and Kashyap and Stein (1995) note that the bank lending channel is not operative if banks have access to external sources of funding. The appendix illustrates these relationships with a simple model. This paper provides institutional and empirical evidence that the money multiplier and the associated narrow bank lending channel are not relevant for analyzing the United States.

---

[1] It is important *not* to interpret the above result as the 'liquidity puzzle.' The Fed can and does affect total balances by changing interest rates. However, the flow of events is different. When the FOMC changes its monetary policy stance (say by raising the funds rate target), demand for reserve balances declines, which in turn prompts the Fed to reduce total balances via open market operations. There are two things to emphasize: First, the decline in supply of balances follows a demand adjustment (and does not precede it), and second, the Fed's control over broader aggregates is limited to total balances. See Carpenter and Demiralp (2008).

The Money Multiplier: Fact or Fiction?

The most simple money multiplier described in textbooks links reservable deposits to bank reserves according to equation (1):

$$\Delta D = \frac{1}{r} \Delta R \qquad (1)$$

where ΔR refers to changes in total reserves, ΔD refers to changes in reservable deposits, r is the required reserves ratio, and $\frac{1}{r}$ is the simple multiplier. Open market purchases increase the quantity of reserves, because of fractional reserve accounting, banks can lend out extra funds, and the extra lending increases both lending and the money supply because loans are created as demand deposits. Money increases by $1/r$ and lending increases by $(1-r)/r$. The story is symmetric, so contractionary policy works in precisely the opposite direction.

The upper panel in Figure 1 plots the theoretical simple multiplier, $\frac{1}{r}$ (black bars) against the actual multiplier implied by the data, $\frac{\Delta D}{\Delta R}$ (gray bars), where deposits are measured as reservable deposits with data from 1990 to 2008.[2] The constant required reserves ratio since 1992 leads to a constant theoretical multiplier after that year. The actual ratio of changes in total reserves to reservable deposits, in contrast, was rather volatile in that period and generally greater than the simple multiplier.

During the financial crisis, the divergence has been even greater. Reserve balances have recently increased dramatically, going from around $15 billion in July 2007 to over $788 billion in December 2008. Despite this increase by a factor of 50, no similar increase in any measure of

---

[2] Only transactions accounts have required reserve ratios above zero during the sample period. Constructing a similar multiplier using M2 would show an even greater difference between the theoretical multiplier and the calculated multiplier.

money, as suggested by the multiplier, could be found. Hence, while the actual multiplier was about twice the theoretical multiplier in 2003, it was about 1/50th of the theoretical multiplier in 2008. Considering other measures of money, the monetary base, the narrowest definition of money, doubled over that period while M2 grew by only 8½ percent.[3]

Casual empirical evidence points away from a standard money multiplier and away from a story in which monetary policy has a direct effect on broader monetary aggregates. The explanation lies in the institutional structure in the United States, especially after 1990. First, there is no direct link between reserves and money—as defined as M2. Following a change in required reserves ratios in early 1990s, reserve requirements are assessed on only about one-tenth of M2.[4] Second, there is no direct link between money—defined as M2—and bank lending. Banks have access to non-deposit funding (and such liabilities would also not be reservable), so the narrow bank lending channel breaks down in theory. Notably, large time deposits, a liability that banks are able to manage more directly to fund loans, are not reservable and not included in M2. Banks' ability to issue managed liabilities increased substantially in the period after 1990, following the developments and increased liquidity in the markets for bank liabilities. Furthermore, the removal of interest rate ceilings through Regulation Q significantly improved the ability of banks to generate non-reservable liabilities by offering competitive rates on large time deposits. Additionally, money market mutual funds account for about one-fifth of M2, but

---

[3] The simple multiplier abstracts from excess reserves and currency. A more general but perhaps less rigorously derived multiplier links the monetary base to broader monetary aggregates (such as M2) to the monetary base according to: $\Delta M = \frac{1+c}{c+e+r} \Delta MB$ where c is the ratio of currency in circulation to reservable deposits, e is the ratio of excess reserves to reservable deposits, and r is the required reserves ratio. In the special case where $c=e=0$, this version of the money multiplier, reduces to the simple multiplier. The lower panel in Figure 1 shows that the discrepancy between this theoretical money multiplier (black bars) and the implied empirical money multiplier (gray bars) is even greater.

[4] Moreover, OMOs affect Federal Reserve balances owned by the banking sector, not required reserves specifically. We use the term "reserve balances" to denote any balances of depository institutions held at the Federal Reserve. These balances can be required reserve balances, contractual clearing balances, or excess reserve balances. See Carpenter and Demiralp, 2006 for a more extensive discussion.

are not on bank balance sheets, and thus they cannot be used to fund lending. These facts imply that the tight link suggested by the multiplier between reserves and money and bank lending does not exist.

Finally, the assumed link in the textbook version of the money multiplier between the creation of loans and the creation of demand deposits is dubious. According to the standard multiplier theory, an increase in bank lending is associated with an increase in demand deposits. The data as discussed below do not reflect any such link.

Bank Balance Sheets

In discussing the money multiplier, we must first define money. For better or worse, most economists think of M2 as the measure of money. M2 is defined as the sum of currency, checking deposits, savings deposits, retail money market mutual funds, and small time deposits. Since 1992, the only deposits on depository institutions' balance sheets that had reserve requirements have been transaction deposits, which are essentially checking deposits.[5] As noted above, the majority of M2 is not reservable and money market mutual funds are not liabilities of depository institutions. Nevertheless, it is the link between money and reserves that drives the theoretical money multiplier relationship. As a result, the standard multiplier cannot be an important part of the transmission mechanism because reserves are not linked to most of M2.

For perspective, M2 averaged about $7¼ trillion in 2007. In contrast, reservable deposits were about $600 billion, or about 8 percent of M2. Moreover, bank loans for 2007 were about $6¼ trillion.[6] This simple comparison suggests that reservable deposits are in no way sufficient

---

[5] To be precise, some other types of deposits are technically reservable, but their reserve requirement was set to zero.
[6] Indeed, this measure severely understates the discrepancy between reservable deposits and depository credit as it represents only commercial bank credit. Savings banks and other thrifts account for a nontrivial fraction of lending in the United States.

to fund bank lending. Indeed, if we consider the fact that reserve balances held at the Federal Reserve were about $15 billion and required reserves were about $43 billion, the tight link drawn in the textbook transmission mechanism from reserves to money and bank lending seems all the more tenuous. Figure 2 plots required reserves with M2 (both panels), and there is no relationship. M2 trends upward, growing in nominal terms with the economy. Required reserves, however, fell dramatically just after 1990 following the reduction in required reserve ratios and trended down through 2000, largely as retail sweep programs allowed depository institutions to reduce their reserve requirements. The fact that only a very small fraction of M2 is reservable explains the disconnect between money, measured as M2, and required reserves. Bank loans are shown as the dashed line in the upper panel and have a similar trend to that of M2. Of course trending nominal variables will often exhibit spurious correlation, but it is clear that there is no link between reserves and loans.[7]

Further complicating the story is the fact that required reserves and the reserves held by banks at the Federal Reserve, which we refer to as reserve balances, are different concepts.[8] The lower panel in Figure 2 shows the level of reserve balances as the dotted line. It too bears little if any relationship to the pattern of M2. Open market operations adjust the level of reserve balances, so to understand the transmission mechanism, we want to ask if there is a direct link from reserve balances to money or lending. Institutional detail and casual empiricism clearly point away from the textbook money multiplier as a relevant concept for understanding the effects of open market operations on money and bank lending.

---

[7] The fact that part of M2, retail money funds, is not on depository institutions' books is not relevant for this comparison. A graph of M2 excluding money funds would look quite similar.
[8] Again, see Carpenter and Demiralp 2008 for a discussion.

An Empirical Look at the Traditional Transmission Mechanism

We turn now to econometric analysis of the transmission mechanism of monetary policy as a different way to examine the money multiplier. Although the real side of the transmission mechanism is clearly important, the real side has received, and continues to receive, a great deal of attention, and so this paper will not address which sectors of the economy are affected by monetary policy. Nevertheless, to avoid misspecifying endogenous monetary policy in the empirical work, we include standard measures of economic activity. In a similar vein, we do not address the yield-curve implications of the transmission of monetary policy. While these concerns are clearly important, our focus is a bit narrower, examining the transmission mechanism from open market operations to money and bank lending. We appeal to Granger causality tests and vector autoregressions (VARs) to let the data summarize the relationships involved.

Aggregate Analysis at the Monthly Frequency

i) Granger Causality Tests

As a first look at the transmission mechanism, we run some Granger-causality tests of deposits, bank loans, and balances of depository institutions at the Federal Reserve at a monthly frequency. The data appendix provides more detail about these variables. Consider the following aggregated, simplified balance sheet of the banking system:

Assets	Liabilities
Required reserve balances[9]	Reservable deposits
Excess reserve balances	Managed liabilities
	Other liabilities and capital
Applied vault cash	
Surplus vault cash	
Loans	

[9] Here, we combine required reserve balances with required clearing balances.

Securities and other assets

Managed liabilities refer to deposits that can be increased or decreased at will, such as large, or wholesale, time deposits, Eurodollar and other Eurocurrency borrowings, repos, and federal funds purchased to meet a bank's needs for funds to pay off maturing deposits and to fund new loans.

We run the Granger causality tests in both log levels and in differences. The latter is used to avoid the clear nonstationarity problem evident in the charts of M2 and bank loans, however our results are substantially the same under either specification. In considering the effect of an open market operation on bank loans, the changes as well as the level of the variables are of interest in the event that reserve balances are important for the funding of loans at the margin. Open market operations are aimed at changing the level of reserve balances, as distinct from total reserves, so we want to test how that level of reserve balances is determined and what other variables those balances affect. This distinction is also important when considering the increase in reserve balances since the financial crisis.

Table 1 presents results of Granger causality tests. The upper panel shows the results when the variables are in log levels and the lower panel shows the results when the variables are in first differences. Each cell shows the p-values from pairwise Granger causality tests where the dependent variable is shown in the left hand column and the independent variable is the variable indicated in the column heading (1 through 6).[10] If the traditional money multiplier story were valid, we would expect to see changes in required reserves (equal to the sum of required reserves balances and applied vault cash) or reserve balances result in changes in money. The changes in money would then result in changes in bank loans.

---

[10] We also run Granger Causality tests with lags of CPI (in difference form) included for comparability with the previous literature. The results are virtually identical (not shown).

First, we test the direction of Granger causality between required reserves and reserve balances on the one hand and reservable deposits on the other. Given that required reserves are close to a linear function of reservable deposits, it is unsurprising to see that reservable deposits Granger cause reserves (row 1, column 2). If a depository institution's customers deposit more funds in their checking accounts, that depository institution is required to hold a higher level of reserves. Reservable liabilities, essentially deposits subject to reserve requirements, do not Granger cause reserve balances (row 4, column 2) in first differences. In levels, however, these liabilities do Granger cause reserve balances. This finding is neither obvious though it is not especially surprising; when a depository institution's reserve requirement rises, it has the option of satisfying that requirement with either vault cash or balances at the Fed. In the short run, it seems that reserve balances are adjusted. Through time, and reflected in the results for the first differences specification, balances can adjust independently if a depository institution changes its contractual clearing balance or its sweeping arrangements, so there is not a mechanical link between reservable deposits and reserve balances.

As noted by equation (2), the traditional money multiplier story posits that the central bank changes the quantity of reserves through an open market operation. If the level of reserves is increased, the amount of funds that a bank can lend out increases, and concomitantly, the level of reservable deposits increases in line with the change in loans. So, if this channel were operative, we would expect to see a change in reserves cause a change in reservable deposits and a change in loans. Furthermore, we would see a change in loans cause a change in reservable deposits because the multiplier theory assumes that the lender bank puts the loan proceeds into the borrower's checking account. The Granger causality results do not, however, bear out these types of relationships. We cannot reject the hypothesis that reserves do not Granger cause reservable liabilities (row 2, column 1) or loans (row 3, column 1). That is to say, the causality is unidirectional, from deposits to reserves. Similarly, we cannot reject the hypothesis that loans do not Granger cause reservable liabilities (row 2, column 3) either. Interestingly, reservable deposits appear to Granger cause loans (row 3, column 2). Reservable liabilities could be a source of funds for banks, and they can be used to support bank loans. However, the volume of reservable liabilities is simply not sufficient to meet the funding needs for bank loans at the aggregate level, and banks meet the rest of their funding needs by issuing managed liabilities. In fact, when we compare the changes in reservable deposits to changes in loans (not shown), we observe that changes in the former are generally about an order of magnitude smaller relative to changes in loans. This observation also holds when we lag the series relative to each other. Meanwhile, changes in managed liabilities are comparable to changes in loans. Hence, we claim that reservable liabilities cannot be driving loans and that the marginal funding source of lending is not reservable liabilities.

At this point, we feel reasonably confident that there is little evidence that open market operations can directly change loans by changing deposits. It must be the case, however, that as assets on a bank's balance sheet change, liabilities must also change. A more plausible channel is that the quantity of loans is primarily determined by the demand, which is presumably a function of price and other economic variables, subject to the borrower meeting the criteria set forth by the bank. To fund these loans, banks have a set of liabilities that they can adjust in reaction to shifts in the demand for loans. If this characterization is accurate, these managed liabilities and loans should move together, but the ability to distinguish between statistical causality and true causality is difficult (we address this issue in more detail in the next section). That said, we can see that changes in both managed liabilities and its sub-category large time deposits Granger cause loans (row 3, columns 5 and 6). Meanwhile, changes in loans do not Granger cause managed liabilities but large time deposits (rows 5 and 6, column 3). Because loans and managed liabilities in a real sense represent two sides of a balance sheet, they might be expected to covary.

ii) Vector Autoregression Analysis

In this section we consider VAR analysis to investigate the role of deposits played in the monetary transmission mechanism at the aggregate level. We first consider a simple extension of the model developed in Bernanke and Blinder (1992). In order to explore the role of funds rate in the monetary transmission mechanism, Bernanke and Blinder estimate a monthly, six-variable VAR with the federal funds rate, consumer price index, bank loans, total deposits, bank securities, and the unemployment rate. All of the financial quantity variables are in log form and are normalized by the consumer price index. We decompose bank liabilities into reservable deposits and managed liabilities because the multiplier story hinges on the different nature of these two types of liabilities in the loan generation process. We consider six lags, as in Bernanke and Blinder. Our sample period covers January 1990 to June 2007, which corresponds to the most recent interest rate targeting regime.[11] We intentionally excluded data from the financial crisis. Changes to the financial system were extreme and liquidity risk was seen as a particularly important aspect of banks' decision making. As a result, the large runup in reserve balances with a pullback in lending would bias our results against the money multiplier.

Figure 3 shows the results from the impulse response analysis to a funds rate shock. Variables in the figure appear in the Choleski order, assuming that the funds rate affects the

---

[11] While the Federal Reserve started to announce changes in the funds rate explicitly after February 1994, the interest rate targeting regime started in late 1980s (see Meulendyke, 1988, and Carpenter and Demiralp, 2008)

macroeconomic variables contemporaneously but it is not affected by them within the same month. Nevertheless the results are virtually unchanged under alternative orderings. Total loans increase in the first year following a positive shock to funds rate, in contrast to Bernanke and Blinder's findings for an earlier sample period (1959-1978) where total loans declined significantly following a monetary tightening (Figure 4). The likely explanation is from the credit channel literature. Following a monetary tightening, it is harder for businesses to obtain non-bank sources of funding, and therefore demand for bank loans may increase. In the post-1990 sample, an increasing share of bank loans is made under a previous commitment. That is, sometime in the past, the borrower and the bank make an agreement on terms of a loan and the borrower has the option on when to take it out, see Morgan (1998). During a tightening cycle, as terms and standards on all borrowing becomes more restrictive, borrowers may call in these previous commitments and there may be a consequent increase in bank loans even though the rest of the economy may be slowing.[12]

While it is difficult to know exactly how much the magnitude of loan commitments changed over time, we can infer this information indirectly. The Survey of Terms of Business Lending notes that the percentage of C&I loans made under commitment remained stable around 70 to 80 percent from 1982 through 2008.[13] Combining this information with the positive trend in C&I loans over that sample period (not shown), one can conclude that total loans under commitment increased significantly over the last decade, which was not prevalent in Bernanke and Blinder's sample.

---

[12] In a recent paper, Ivashina and Scharfstein (2008) underlined this phenomenon by pointing to the rise in commercial and industrial (C&I) loans around the bankruptcy of Lehman Brothers during the recent financial turmoil. They noted that companies rushed for their revolving credit facilities when they think that credit conditions will tighten in the near future.
[13] Federal Reserve statistical release E2.

The gradual change in the behavior of bank loans and the rising role of loan commitments can be observed more clearly when we restrict the analysis to the 1959-1978 sample period considered by Bernanke and Blinder (Figure 4). For this sample, we substitute large time deposits (Deposits_Lg) for managed liabilities because the data for the latter are only available after 1988. Here, we do not observe any increase in bank loans following a tightening, and hence, there is no consequent increase in large time deposits to fund such loans.

Going back to Figure 3, the responses of reservable deposits and managed liabilities following a shock to the funds rate are also consistent with the story told above. Reservable deposits decline following the increase in the funds rate, likely due to the increase in the opportunity cost of holding checking accounts, similar to the response of total deposits in Bernanke and Blinder. However, managed liabilities rise following the increase in the funds rate because banks need to fund the increase in loans by issuing more managed liabilities. At the end of about two years, managed liabilities return to their original value, just around the same time when bank loans return to their original value. The multiplier story would suggest a decline in loans, following the decline in reservable deposits after a monetary tightening. Clearly, this is not the case; banks simply raise more external funding to finance their loans.

Traditionally, studies that investigate the monetary transmission mechanism face the difficulty of identifying whether the change in loans is due to demand (the interest-rate or money channel) or supply (credit channel) following a monetary policy action. For our purposes, however, the type of change in supply that we are trying to examine is a change in the quantity of reserves. In this sample period, a decline in reservable deposits is associated with an increase in loan supply. The evidence clearly suggests that the narrow bank lending channel is not functional at the aggregate level for the period after 1990.

Figure 5 investigates the determinants of bank loans in more detail. The upper panel shows that managed liabilities rise immediately in response to an increase in bank loans whereas the increase in reservable deposits is barely significant and short-lived, reinforcing the notion that it is managed liabilities that fund a substantial portion of lending. Because these liabilities are not subject to reserve requirements, the textbook story of the money multiplier cannot be the operative channel of policy transmission. Bank loans rise slightly in response to an increase in managed liabilities (lower right panel). These patterns may be simple correlation that is imperfectly identified by the ordering in the VAR. Regardless, there is a clear link between managed liabilities and loans. In contrast, bank loans move in the wrong direction following a shock to reservable deposits (lower left panel). If we take these results completely literally, bank loans increase rather than decrease in response to a decrease in reservable deposits. Recall that the multiplier story presumed that bank loans increase significantly in response to any increase in reservable deposits, and our results clearly illustrate that this is not the case.[14]

Impulse response functions are useful summaries of the reaction of variables to shocks to other variables. Another potentially useful metric of the impact of reserves on money and bank lending is to look at the variance decomposition from VARs. The first two columns of Table 2 show the percentage of the forecast error in bank loans explained by reservable deposits and managed liabilities (the rest of the variables included in the VAR are not shown). The two variables have comparable predictive power in explaining bank loans. The last two columns show the variance decomposition analysis from an alternative VAR where managed liabilities

---

[14] Another way to check whether bank loans respond to reserve supply is to consider the identification strategy introduced by Strongin (1995) to distinguish between reserve supply shocks and reserve demand shocks. Strongin assumes that reserve demand is inelastic at the monthly frequency due to the pre-determined nature of reserve requirements and the demand for excess reserves. Under this assumption, when total reserves are ordered prior to non-borrowed reserves in a Choleski ordering, shocks to non-borrowed reserves capture reserve supply shocks. As an additional test for our argument, we added total reserves and non-borrowed reserves to our VAR system. The response of bank loans to a shock to non-borrowed reserves was insignificant, consistent with the rest of our findings (not shown).

are replaced by large time deposits.[15] The difference between the explanatory powers of reservable and non-reservable deposits is more noticeable when we use this sub-component of managed liabilities. It is also important to note that these results are obtained despite the fact that managed liabilities or large time deposits are ordered after reservable deposits. These findings suggest that changes to the balance sheet from managed liabilities are more important than changes in deposits that are linked to the money multiplier.

iii) Counterfactual Experiments

In Figure 3, we documented an increase in bank loans in response to contractionary monetary policy, possibly as customers draw on previously committed credit lines. We argued that banks support this increase in bank loans by increasing their managed liabilities despite a decline in reservable liabilities; we consider that pattern to be evidence against the traditional bank lending channel. Another way of understanding the role of reservable deposits and managed liabilities in funding bank loans is to consider what happens to impulse response functions when their roles are independently suppressed by setting their coefficients at the current and all lagged values to zero. The difference between the actual impulse-response function and this counterfactual impulse response function should measure the work that each variable does in the VAR. If a variable has a significant role in funding bank loans, the impulse-response function with its action suppressed should be significantly different from the original one. This type of an exercise may also shed light into the true causal structure between bank loans and liabilities.

In the first counterfactual experiment, we suppress managed liabilities or reservable deposits and observe the behavior of bank loans to a funds rate shock. Figure 6 shows the results

---

[15] The impulse response analysis from this VAR specification is very similar to the original specification in Figure 3.

from this exercise. In this figure, the solid line replicates the original impulse response function in Figure 3, while the line with hollow circles and the line with stars plot the impulse response functions with managed liabilities and reservable deposits suppressed respectively. Because all three impulse response functions lie within the 95 percent confidence interval, we note that the three functions are not significantly different from each other, suggesting that the increase in bank loans following a funds rate shock is not due to a change in bank liabilities. This result is consistent with our argument that the increase in bank loans following a monetary tightening is driven by demand side pressures due to loan commitments.

Figure 6 suggests that the causal direction between bank loans and liabilities does not go from liabilities to loans. Does it go the other way round? Do banks raise their managed liabilities when faced with an increase in loan demand? In order to address this question, we need to investigate whether an increase in loans leads to an increase in managed liabilities. The upper panel in Figure 7 looks at the response of managed liabilities to a funds rate shock. Once again, the solid line replicates the response of managed liabilities in Figure 3. When bank loans are kept constant, the increase in managed liabilities lies significantly below the original impulse response function in the second half of the year. In other words, the increase in managed liabilities that we have observed in Figure 3 seems to be related to the increase in loan demand. Faced with an increase in total loans, banks raise more managed liabilities to fund these loans. Hence, the causality seems to flow from loans to liabilities. What about reservable deposits? Banks do not have an active role in controlling reservable deposits because their customers tend to determine how much money to keep in these accounts. Therefore, the response of reservable deposits is not expected to be different when we suppress bank loans. Indeed, the lower panel in

Figure 7 shows that that the impulse response function from the counterfactual experiment is not significantly different from the original impulse response function.

The message that we get from Figure 7 is that following a monetary tightening, managed liabilities do not increase as much when bank loans are suppressed. Nevertheless, there is still a significant rise in the first six months following a tightening. What other variable besides bank loans could explain this increase? The most likely candidate is deposit rates embedded in the funds rate shock. Interest rates offered on large time deposits are set competitively to adjust the volume of external funding. Hence, when faced with an increase in loans, it is plausible to expect banks to increase the rates offered on large time deposits to raise their volume. In that respect, the counterfactual experiment in the upper panel of Figure 7 fails to control for the entire influence of loan demand on managed liabilities because the funds rate shock itself may reflect the increase in deposit rates.

Our last exercise adds the interest rate offered on six-month CDs to the VAR.[16] The CD rate is ordered after the funds rate, implying that banks can adjust the rates offered on these CDs within the same month as the Fed's policy action. The impulse response analysis from this VAR looks very similar to Figure 3 and the response of CD rate follows the same path as the funds rate as we would expect (not shown).[17] In the counterfactual experiment, we first suppress the CD rate to evaluate the role played by the CD rate alone. The upper panel in Figure 8 shows the response of managed liabilities. The increase in managed liabilities declines if the CD rate is kept constant but the difference is mostly insignificant. The lower panel in Figure 8 suppresses the CD rate together with bank loans. This time, we observe that managed liabilities hardly change in response to a monetary policy action. This is strongly supportive of our underlying

---

[16] Considering CD rates with alternative maturities do not change the qualitative results (not shown).
[17] Once again, the results are not sensitive to alternative orderings.

argument that managed liabilities (and not reservable deposits) are used as the marginal source of funds for bank loans.

Aggregate Analysis at the Quarterly Frequency

In this section, we repeat the VAR exercise at the quarterly frequency. One virtue of working at this frequency is that there are data on total domestic non-financial borrowing at this frequency. In the previous section, we argued that the increase in bank loans following a monetary tightening may be due to a decrease in non-bank sources of funding. If non-bank funding does become more scarce, we would expect total borrowing to decrease (or remain constant) following a tightening even though bank loans may increase. Because total borrowing data is only available at a quarterly frequency, we consider a VAR at this frequency and also add data on GDP and the GDP deflator to fully capture the policy maker's reaction function. The structural VAR is identified with the following Choleski ordering: Unemployment rate, GDP, GDP deflator, required reserves, loans, total nonfinancial borrowing, reservable deposits, managed liabilities, securities, and funds rate. Nominal variables, which are in log form, are normalized by the GDP deflator. Macroeconomic variables are ordered first and the funds rate is ordered last because the funds rate is expected to respond to these variables contemporaneously at a quarterly frequency. Our robustness checks reveal that the results are not sensitive to alternative orderings (not shown). The VAR is estimated with two lags consistent with six lags that were considered in the earlier analysis at a monthly frequency. Figure 9 shows the results from this exercise in response to a funds rate shock. Despite the increase in bank loans following a tightening (second row, first column), there is a decline in total nonfinancial borrowing (second row, second column), a result that is consistent with the asymmetric information problems discussed earlier.

If the multiplier story was accurate, we would expect a monetary tightening to be associated with a decline in bank reserves, which in turn, would reduce reservable deposits. Required reserves exhibit no such decline in Figure 9, and the point estimate is positive through most of the forecast horizon (first row, fourth column).

Disaggregated Quarterly Frequency

Our analysis so far documented evidence that the bank lending channel and the simple money multiplier are not functional at the aggregate level in the post-1990 period. In particular, we have shown that a contractionary monetary policy action is accompanied by an increase (not a decrease) in bank loans and an increase in managed liabilities to fund these loans. Despite the observed decline in securities to a funds rate shock, the combined effect of an increase in loans and a decrease in securities offsets any multiplier effect on broader monetary aggregates. Are these findings supported across the banking universe? In other words, is the aggregate data driven by a dominant group, or are the results valid across all bank types? If there is a dominant group that has easier access to external finance, does bank size, bank liquidity (see Kashyap and Stein, 2000), bank capital (see Kishan and Opiela, 2000), or a combination of these factors characterize this group? In order to answer these questions, we move to bank level data and maintain the same VAR methodology from the previous section. This way, we are able to compare the micro level evidence with macro evidence and pinpoint the underlying differences.

Bank-Level Data

Our source for all bank level data is the Consolidated Report of Condition and Income (known as the Call Reports) that insured banks submit each quarter. The data are reported on a quarter-end basis. The main challenge of working with Call Report data is that the data are designed primarily for regulatory purposes rather than research purposes. We employ the filters adopted by the previous researchers (Kashyap and Stein, 2000, Den Haan, Sumner, and Yamashiro, 2007) to clean up the data and form consistent time series. Because there is a break in total securities series in 1994, we start our sample in 1994:Q1 and end it shortly before the beginning of the crisis in 2007:Q2.[18] We use large time deposits as a proxy for managed liabilities and transaction deposits as a proxy for reservable deposits. The data are gathered at the individual bank level. The data appendix describes the construction of our key series in detail.[19]

Table 3 examines the balance sheets for banks of different sizes. There are two panels corresponding to the starting and the ending points of our sample. The size categories are defined following Kashyap and Stein (2000): banks below the 75th percentile by asset size, banks between 75th and 90th percentiles, banks between the 90th and 95th percentiles, banks between the 95th and 98th percentiles, and banks above the 99th percentile. What is interesting for our purposes is that despite the larger share of transaction deposits relative to large time deposits across all size categories in the earlier sample (more than three times as much), the relative share of large time deposits increased substantially as the share of transaction deposits declined by the end of the sample. As of 2007:Q2, large time deposits exceed the share of

---

[18] Our results with the aggregate data remain mostly unchanged when we restrict the sample to the post-1994 period, although the increase in total loans is less pronounced.

[19] Kashyap and Stein (2000) use the consolidated total loan series in their analysis (RCFD 1400), whereas Den Haan et al. (2002) suggest the use of domestic total loan series (RCON 1400) because the consolidated series displays discontinuity. While we report the results with domestic total loans series, our results remain virtually identical if we use the consolidated series.

transaction deposits in all size categories except for the smallest size category. This information alone suggests that banks' ability to raise large time deposits increased drastically over the last decade consistent with our earlier discussion about changes to the regulatory environment. The narrow bank lending channel, then, would appear to be ruled out because banks rely on these deposits at the margin rather than transaction deposits to fund new loans.

Table 4 displays alternative breakdowns with respect to the ratio of securities to assets (upper panel) and the ratio of equity to assets (lower panel) respectively. Note that these distributions are not as skewed as the distribution with respect to asset size, and the most liquid or well-capitalized banks are not necessarily the largest banks with respect to asset size. However, no matter how we divide the banks, the share of large time deposits exceed transaction deposits as of the second quarter of 2007.

In order to test whether our VAR evidence at the aggregate level is driven by large banks, we first group banks into three size categories as in Kashyap and Stein (2000): the smallest one contains all banks with total assets below the 95th percentile, the middle one includes banks from the 95th to 99th percentiles, and the largest one has those banks above the 99th percentile. We place each bank into one of these size groups in each quarter. If a bank experiences a substantial change in its asset size (either due to a merger or a persistent change in its growth rate), then it switches to a different size category and stays there indefinitely unless it experiences another major change in future quarters.[20]

We consider a panel VAR to exploit the bank level data and yet preserve our methodology from the previous section. Our quarterly VAR (using quarter-end values) includes

---

[20] In addition to these enduring changes across size categories, a bank may potentially oscillate between size groups if it is a borderline case with respect to the asset size. These temporary fluctuations are dropped from estimation. Specifically, if a particular bank switches to a different size category for less than three quarters, then it will not have sufficient history to have two lags for the VAR estimation and will be automatically dropped from the sample.

the federal funds rate, GDP deflator, securities, loans, transaction deposits, large time deposits, and the unemployment rate. Balance sheet variables are normalized by the GDP deflator and are in log form. We maintain the ordering from our monthly analysis although the results are not sensitive to different orderings.[21] The two differences with respect to the monthly analysis are that the CPI is replaced by the percentage change in the GDP deflator, and the aggregate unemployment rate is replaced by the state-level unemployment rate. In the panel analysis, we control for bank-specific fixed effects. Because fixed effects are correlated with the regressors due to lags of the dependent variables, the mean-differencing procedure that is generally used to eliminate fixed effects creates a bias in the coefficients. Therefore, we use forward-mean differencing following Arellano and Bover (1995). The system is estimated by Generalized Method of Moments (GMM), using lagged regressors as instruments following Love and Zicchino (2006).

Figure 10 shows the impulse response functions with respect to a one standard deviation shock to the funds rate for three bank size categories. It is plausible to expect contractionary monetary policy to be more binding for smaller banks because "these banks are least likely to be able to frictionlessly raise uninsured finance" (Kasyhap and Stein, 2000, p. 409). However, looking at the response of bank loans to a funds rate shock (row one), we notice that the increase in bank loans is clearly not driven by large banks, as one might expect. In fact, bank loans decline initially following a contractionary shock and hover around zero for large and medium banks (columns one and two) whereas they increase substantially for small banks (column three). If small banks had difficulties in raising nonreservable deposits, and if bank loans were indeed a dependent on transaction deposits, then Kashyap and Stein's characterization of small banks

---

[21] We use the last day of the quarter value for the federal funds rate and the last month of the quarter value for the GDP deflator.

would make them unable to meet the increase in loan demand; the data, though, show that this is not the case. The empirical evidence is thus clearly aligned against the traditional belief about the workings of the money multiplier and the narrow bank lending channel. Instead, it seems to be the case that small banks sell securities and issue large time deposits to offset the decline in their transaction deposits and meet the increased demand for loans. The decline in bank loans in other bank sizes may suggest that the customers of smaller banks have a greater tendency to use their loan commitments relative to the customers of larger banks.

If bank size alone does not determine a bank's ability to raise nonreservable deposits, what other factors could? Our next experiment is to consider the role of liquidity in generating nonreservable deposits. We measure liquidity by the ratio of securities to assets as in Kashyap and Stein (2000). We group banks based on whether their securities to assets ratio is less than 20 percent (least liquid), between 20 and 30 percent (liquid), and more than 30 percent (most liquid) in each quarter. This classification divides the sample into three comparable sized bins.[22]

Kashyap and Stein (2000) note that the smallest, most illiquid banks are the most responsive to monetary policy. Our previous findings suggest that bank size does not appear to be a restriction in bank lending behavior, at least for the period after 1990. What about liquidity? Figure 11a shows the impulse response functions to a funds rate shock for three liquidity groups. Looking at the response of bank loans to a funds rate shock, we observe that the least liquid banks are most affected by the contractionary shock. Indeed, the response of bank loans (row 1) is mostly negative for the least liquid banks (column one), declines after the third quarter for the liquid banks (column two), and it is entirely positive for the most liquid banks (column three).

---

[22] We have a total of 158,297 bank quarters in the least liquid bank group, 119,134 bank quarters in the liquid bank group, and 159,844 bank quarters in the most liquid bank group.

In these results, there is some evidence that funding is not completely frictionless and that a bank's balance sheet does, in fact matter. Our results, therefore, are not out of the mainstream. Nevertheless, it is not entirely clear what is behind the decline in bank loans for the less liquid banks. We need to investigate the response of other components to identify the underlying reason. Looking across the liquidity categories, we note that all three groups experience a persistent decline in transaction deposits following a contractionary policy shock (row two), and all three groups try to offset this decline in liabilities by raising large time deposits (row three). However, the extent of the increase in large time deposits varies across categories, likely reflecting their relative needs for funding. For example, the least liquid banks are more aggressive in raising large time deposits. They also tend to reduce securities holdings less than other banks (row four). Note that the banks with the least liquid balance sheets do not decrease their securities as much, while the banks with the most liquid balance sheets sell off their securities more than the other banks to keep their loan portfolio intact.

The first two rows in Figure 11b confirm our findings at the aggregate level that bank loans are primarily driven by large time deposits. Similarly, the relationship between bank loans and transaction deposits is negative for the least liquid banks who had experienced a decline in their loans (row four), in contrast to the predictions of the bank lending channel. Clearly, if the decline in bank loans for these banks was due to a decline in reservable deposits, we would expect loans to respond positively to a shock in transaction deposits. A negative and significant relationship as displayed in row four cannot be consistent with the bank lending channel and suggests that it is the demand side that drives the response of loans to monetary policy.

Row three indicates that banks try to offset the decline in reservable deposits by raising nonreservable deposits. While banks in all three liquidity categories raise significantly more large time deposits to shield against the loss in reservable deposits, the negative relationship is most pronounced for the least liquid banks, likely because these banks cannot sell enough securities to offset the decline in their liabilities and insulate their balance sheet from the contractionary cycle. Because banks respond to a decline in transaction deposits by selling off their securities, there is a positive relationship between these variables (row five), the extent of which strengthens with the liquidity of the bank.

Our last experiment considers grouping banks based on their capital leverage ratios. It may be argued that banks with higher capital ratios have less difficulty in raising nonreservable funds and hence they should be able to insulate their balance sheets from monetary policy actions (see for example Kashyap and Stein (2000) and Kishan and Opelia (2000)). Following Kishan and Opelia (2000), we focus on the equity capital to total asset ratios and form the groups as: <8 percent (undercapitalized), ≥8 and <10 percent (adequately capitalized), and ≥10 percent (well-capitalized) in each quarter. Once again, the relative sizes of the three groups are comparable.[23] Figure 12 shows the impulse responses to a funds rate shock for the three groups. Similar to the breakdown with respect to liquidity, we note that the well capitalized banks (column 3) supply more loans, while adequately capitalized (column 2) and undercapitalized banks (column 1) experience mostly a decline in their loans following a contraction (row 1). In contrast to the picture presented Figure 11a, all three groups in Figure 12 reduce their securities to offset the decline in liabilities because there are no systematic differences in securities holdings between the three groups (row four). As a result, the responses of large time deposits also resemble each other across the three groups, where banks in all groups raise their large time deposits. The impulse response functions for the rest of the variables are very similar to our

---

[23] We have a total of 104,909 bank quarters in the undercapitalized group, 153,601 bank quarters in the adequately capitalized group, and 178,766 bank quarters in the well capitalized group.

findings in Figure 11b (not shown). In particular, the response of bank loans to transaction deposits is negative or non-existent for all categories. If banks with lower capital ratios indeed reduced bank loans because they had trouble raising non-reservable deposits, we would find a positive response of bank loans to transaction deposits. Once again, our findings argue against the existence of a narrow bank lending channel.

Evaluation of Panel VAR Analysis

Our analysis at the bank level supports our findings at the aggregate level that bank loans are simply not funded by reservable deposits at the margin and suggests that the bank lending channel is not functional, no matter how we group the banks. The observed differences in the response of bank loans to monetary policy seem to be driven by demand factors. Less liquid and undercapitalized banks observe a decline in bank loans and securities following a contractionary shock. While the decline in bank loans is not due to the decline in transaction deposits, the decline in securities does seem to be associated with the decline in transaction deposits. Some variant of the money multiplier, then, may be operative only for these banks. For the more liquid and well-capitalized banks, the increase in bank loans counteracts a decline in securities and offsets any multiplier effect.

The results from the aggregate data seem to be driven by the most liquid or well-capitalized banks. A priori, it is hard to see why this is necessarily the case, given that these banks do not constitute a larger share in the universe of all banks, as indicated in Table 4. While the aggregate balance sheet data are based on the Call Reports, the bank credit data comes from bank credit reports submitted to the Federal Reserve (Board of Governors, H.8. Statistical

Release). Our results suggest that perhaps a larger percentage of these reporters have higher securities or equity relative to their assets.

Conclusions

The role of reserves and money in macroeconomics has a long history. Simple textbook treatments of the money multiplier give the quantity of bank reserves a causal role in determining the quantity of money and bank lending and thus the transmission mechanism of monetary policy. This role results from the assumptions that reserve requirements generate a direct and tight linkage between money and reserves and that the central bank controls the money supply by adjusting the quantity of reserves through open market operations. Using data from recent decades, we have demonstrated that this simple textbook link is implausible in the United States for a number of reasons. First, when money is measured as M2, only a small portion of it is reservable and thus only a small portion is linked to the level of reserve balances the Fed provides through open market operations. Second, except for a brief period in the early 1980s, the Fed has traditionally aimed to control the federal funds rate rather than the quantity of reserves. Third, reserve balances are not identical to required reserves, and the federal funds rate is the interest rate in the market for all reserve balances, not just required reserves. Reserve balances are supplied elastically at the target funds rate. Finally, reservable liabilities fund only a small fraction of bank lending and the evidence suggests that they are not the marginal source of funding, either. All of these points are a reflection of the institutional structure of the U.S. banking system and suggest that the textbook role of money is not operative.

While the institutional facts alone provide compelling support for our view, we also demonstrate empirically that the relationships implied by the money multiplier do not exist in the data for the most liquid and well-capitalized banks. Changes in reserves are unrelated to changes in lending, and open market operations do not have a direct impact on lending. We conclude that the textbook treatment of money in the transmission mechanism can be rejected. Specifically, our results indicate that bank loan supply does not respond to changes in monetary policy through a bank lending channel, no matter how we group the banks.

Our evidence against the bank lending channel at the aggregate level is consistent with other recent studies such as Black, Hancock, and Passmore (2007), who reach a similar conclusion about the limited scope of the bank lending channel in the United States, and Cetorelli and Goldberg (2008), who point out the importance of globalization as a way to insulate the banks from domestic monetary policy shocks. Our findings are also consistent with the predictions of Bernanke and Gertler (1995) from over a decade ago that the importance of the traditional bank lending channel would likely diminish over time as depository institutions gained easier access to external funding.

Our evidence against the bank lending channel at the micro level is consistent with Oliner and Rudebusch (1995), but it contrasts previous findings of a lending channel for small, illiquid, or undercapitalized banks (see Kashyap and Stein (2000), Kishan and Opiela, (2000) and Jayartne and Morgan (2000)). What is common in all these studies is that their sample periods cover the period prior to 1995, when reservable deposits constituted the largest source of funding. As we have shown in Table 3, this is no longer a feature that characterizes bank balance sheets in the post-1994 period. Furthermore, Kashyap and Stein (2000) and Kishan and Opiela (2000) interpret a change in the sensitivity of bank lending to monetary policy as evidence of a bank lending channel. We argue that changes in the sensitivity of bank loans may stem from the demand side, and that a better test for the lending channel is to check whether bank loans are financed by reservable deposits. Our findings suggest that this is not the case.

In general, our results echo Romer and Romer (1990)'s version of the Modigliani-Miller theorem for banking firms. They argue that banks are indifferent between reservable deposits and non-reservable deposits. Hence, shocks to reservable deposits do not affect their lending decisions, and changes to reserves only serve to alter the mix of reservable and non-reservable deposits. Our findings in this paper support the argument that shocks to reservable deposits do not change banks' lending decisions.

Since 2008, the Federal Reserve has supplied an enormous quantity of reserve balances relative to historical levels as a result of a set of nontraditional policy actions. These actions were taken to stabilize short-term funding markets and to provide additional monetary policy stimulus at a time when the federal funds rate was at its effective lower bound. The question arises whether or not this unprecedented rise in reserve balances ought to lead to a sharp rise in money and lending. The results in this paper suggest that the quantity of reserve balances itself is not likely to trigger a rapid increase in lending. To be sure, the low level of interest rates could stimulate demand for loans and lead to increased lending, but the narrow, textbook money multiplier does not appear to be a useful means of assessing the implications of monetary policy for future money growth or bank lending.

References

Arellano, Manuel, and Olympia Bover. 1995. "Another look at the instrumental variable estimation of error component models." *Journal of Econometrics*, 68: 29–51.

Bernanke, Ben, and Alan Blinder. 1988. "Credit, Money, and Aggregate Demand." *American Economic Review*, 78: 435-439.

Bernanke, Ben, and Alan Blinder. 1992. "The Federal Funds Rate and the Channels of Monetary Transmission." *American Economic Review*, 82(4): 901-921.

Bernanke, Ben, and Mark Gertler. 1995. "Inside the Black Box: The Credit Channel of Monetary Policy Transmission." *Journal of Economic Perspectives*, 9 (4): 27-48.

Black, Lamont, Diana Hancock, and Wayne Passmore. 2007. "Bank Core Deposits and the Mitigation of Monetary Policy." *Finance and Economics Discussion Series, 2007-65. Board of Governors of the Federal Reserve System.*

Carpenter Seth, and Selva Demiralp. 2008. "The Liquidity Effect at the Federal Funds Market: Evidence at the Monthly Frequency." *Journal of Money, Credit, and Banking*, 40: 1-24.

Cetorelli, Nicola, and Linda Goldberg. 2008. "Bank Globalization, Monetary Transmission, and the Lending Channel," *mimeo, Federal Reserve Bank of New York.*

Den Haan, Wouter, Steven Sumner, and Guy Yamashiro. 2002. "Construction of Aggregate and Regional Bank Data Using the Call Reports: Data Manual," www.csulb.edu/~gyamashi/manual.pdf.

Diamond, Douglas, and Rajan, Raghuram. 2006. "Money in a Theory of Banking." *American Economic Review*, 96: 30-53.

Freeman, Scott, and Kydland, Finn. 2000. "Monetary Aggregates and Output." *American Economic Review*, 90: 1125-1135.

Hafer, Rik, Haslag, Joseph, and Jones, Garett. 2007. "On Money and Output: Is Money Redundant?" *Journal of Monetary Economics*, 54 (3): 945-954.

Hamilton, James. 1997. "Measuring the Liquidity Effect." *American Economic Review*, 87(1): 80-97.

Ireland, Peter. 2004. "Money's Role in the Monetary Business Cycle." *Journal of Money, Credit, and Banking*, 36: 969-983.

Ivashina, Victoria, and David Scharfstein. 2008. "Lending During the Financial Crisis of 2008." www.people.hbs.edu/dscharfstein/Lending_During_the_Crisis.pdf.

Jayarante, Jith, and Donald Morgan. 2000. "Capital Market Frictions and Deposit Constraints at Banks," *Journal of Money, Credit, and Banking*, 32: 74-92.

Kashyap, Anil and Jeremy Stein. 1995. "The Impact of Monetary Policy on Bank Balance Sheets." *Carnegie-Rochester Conference Series on Public Policy*, 42: 151-195.

Kashyap, Anil, and Jeremy Stein. 2000. "What Do a Million Observations on Banks say About the Transmission of Monetary Policy?" *American Economic Review*, 90: 407-428.

Kishan, Ruby, and Timothy Opiela. 2000. "Bank Size, Bank Capital, and the Bank Lending Channel," *Journal of Money, Credit, and Banking*, 32: 121-141.

Kohn, Donald. 2010. "Homework Assignments for Policy Makers," speech at the Cornelson Distinguished Lecture at Davidson College, Davidson, North Carolina, March 24, 2010.

Leeper, Eric, and Jennifer Roush. 2003. "Putting 'M' Back into Monetary Policy." *Journal of Money, Credit, and Banking*, 35: 1217–1256.

Love, Inessa, and Leo Zicchino. 2006. "Financial Development and Dynamic Investment Behavior: Evidence from Panel VAR," *The Quarterly Review of Economics and Finance*, 46: 190–210.

Meulendyke, Ann Marie. 1998. *U.S. Monetary Policy and Financial Markets*, New York, Federal Reserve Bank of New York.

Meltzer, Alan. 2001. "Money and Monetary Policy: An Essay in Honor of Darryl Francis." Federal Reserve Bank of St. Louis, *Review*, July/August: 23-31.

Morgan Donald. 1998. "The Credit Effects of Monetary Policy: Evidence Using Loan Commitments." *Journal of Money Credit and Banking*, 30: 102-118.

Oliner, Steve, and Glenn Rudebusch. 1995. "Is There a Bank Lending Channel for Monetary Policy?" *Federal Reserve Bank of San Francisco Economic Review*, 2: 3-20.

Romer, Christina, and David Romer. 1990. "New Evidence on the Monetary Transmission Mechanism," *Brookings Papers on Economic Activity*, 149-198

Strongin, Steve. 1995. "The Identification of Monetary Policy Disturbances. Explaining the Liquidity Puzzle," *Journal of Monetary Economics* 35, 463-497.

Data Appendix

Aggregate Data

Most of the series were obtained from the Federal Reserve Board. The specifics for each series are provided below.

Required Reserves: H.3 Release, Aggregate Reserves of Depository Institutions and the Monetary Base

Reservable Deposits: Demand Deposits (H.6 release, Components of M1) +Other Checkable Deposits (H.6. release, Components of M1)[24]

Bank Loans: Total Loans and Leases (H.8 release, Assets and Liabilities of Commercial Banks in the United States)

Total Balances: Reserve Balances with Federal Reserve Banks (H.4.1. Release, Factors Affecting Reserve Balances)

Managed Liabilities: Large time deposits (H.6 release, Components of Non-M2 M3) + Net due to related foreign offices (H.8 release, Assets and Liabilities of Commercial Banks in the United States)+ Borrowings from other nonbanks (H.8 release, Assets and Liabilities of Commercial Banks in the United States).

Large Time Deposits: H.6 release, Components of Non-M2 M3

Securities: H.8 release, Assets and Liabilities of Commercial Banks in the United States

Federal Funds Rate: Effective Federal Funds Rate (H.15 Release, Selected Interest Rates)

Six Month CD rate: Bank Rate Monitor

---

[24] Our reservable deposits data consists of demand deposits and other checkable deposits, the former being held exclusively at commercial banks. Moreover, transactions deposits are these two types of deposits adjusted for various other technical factors, such as cash items in the process of collection, but the difference is not material for the purposes of this discussion.

Unemployment Rate: U.S. Department of Labor: Bureau of Labor Statistics. State level unemployment rate data is obtained by the Federal Reserve Bank of Cleveland's web-site.

CPI: Consumer Price Index for all urban consumers: All Items (U.S. Department of Labor: Bureau of Labor Statistics)

GDP Deflator: Federal Reserve Bank of St. Louis, FRED database

Bank Level Data

The following series are obtained from the Call Report series available on the Federal Reserve Bank of Chicago's website. Because there is a break in total securities series (RCFD 0391) from 1994 to 2002, we start our sample in 1994.Q1 and use the sum of total held to maturity series (RCFD 1754) and total available for sale securities (RCFD 1773).

Variable	*MDRM Code and Definition*
Total Assets*	RCFD2170: *TOTAL ASSETS*
Cash	RCFD0010: *CASH AND BALANCES DUE FROM DEPOSITORY INSTITUTIONS*
Securities*	RCFD1754 (*HELD-TO-MATURITY SECURITIES, TOTAL*) +RCFD1773 (*AVAILABLE-FOR-SALE SECURITIES, TOTAL*)
Total Loans*	RCFD1400 (*TOTAL LOANS AND LEASES, GROSS*)
	RCON1400 (*TOTAL LOANS AND LEASES, GROSS*)
Real estate loans	RCFD1410 (*LOANS SECURED BY REAL ESTATE*)
C&I loans	RCFD1600 (*COMMERCIAL AND INDUSTRIAL LOANS (TOTAL LOANS OUTSTANDING)*)

Loans to individuals	RCFD1975 (*LOANS TO INDIVIDUALS FOR HOUSEHOLD, FAMILY, AND OTHER PERSONAL EXPENDITURES*)
Total deposits	RCFD2200 (*TOTAL DEPOSITS*)
Transaction deposits*	RCON2215 (*TOTAL TRANSACTION ACCOUNTS*)
Large deposits*	RCON2604 (*TOTAL TIME DEPOSITS OF $100,000 OR MORE*)
Brokered deposits	RCON2365 (*TOTAL BROKERED DEPOSITS*)
Subordinated debt	RCFD3200 (*SUBORDINATED NOTES AND DEBENTURES*)
Other liabilities	RCFD2170 (*TOTAL ASSETS*) -RCFD2950 (*TOTAL LIABILITIES*)
Equity*	RCFD3210 (*TOTAL EQUITY CAPITAL*)
* Indicates the series that are used in VAR analysis.	

We adopt the following screens to form consistent time series.

1) Banks located within the fifty states and DC (0<RSSD 9210<57).

2) Insured banks (RSSD 9424=1, 2, 6, or 7) where 1 = FDIC/BIF (not valid after 2006.Q1), 2 = FDIC/SAIF(not valid after 2006.Q1), 6 = FDIC/BIF and FDIC/SAIF(not valid after 2006.Q1), and 7 = DIF (Deposit Insurance Fund), (not valid prior to 2006.Q1)

3) Institutions chartered as commercial banks (RSSD=200). In contrast to Kasyhap and Stein (2000) and following Den Haan et al. (2002), we exclude non-deposit trust companies and savings banks from the sample. The excluded banks report on a semi-annual basis. Den Haan et al. note that inclusion of these institutions lead to oscillating series.

4) If any of the series that enter the VAR directly (that is, securities, loans, transaction deposits, large time deposits) or indirectly (that is, assets) have a have a non-positive value, we eliminate that bank from that sample in that period, suspecting that

this is a reporting error. The only exception is bank capital, which is one of the four entries in the Call Reports that is allowed to be negative.

5) For the series that enter the VAR directly or indirectly, observation t of series i is dropped if the growth rate is more than five standard deviations away from the cross sectional mean growth rate of series i in period t.

6) Observation t of series i is included only when four preceding observations are available.

Appendix

A Simple Theoretical Model

In this paper, we tested the existence of a bank lending channel by checking whether or not bank loans are a function of reservable deposits. Our empirical evidence suggested that this is not the case. We argued therefore that a contraction in reservable deposits has no negative impact on bank loans. Instead, bank loans are primarily driven by demand factors. If there is an increase in demand for loans, banks increase their supply of loans (despite a decline in reservable deposits) and obtain the funding by issuing uninsured deposits.

In the context of a simple theoretical model, these claims can be illustrated by showing that the change in bank loans in response to a shock to the supply of reservable deposits is zero where the marginal cost of raising external funds is negligible. Furthermore, the partial derivative of bank loans with respect to a shock to loan demand is positive. In this appendix, we illustrate these claims with the help of a simple model.

The simple theoretical model developed by Jayaratne and Morgan (2000) serves well for our purposes. They consider a case where banks only make loans, L. The marginal revenue from lending is given by $r^L = l_0 - l_1 L$ where l_0 captures loan demand and l_1 is the marginal revenue of lending which is decreasing: $l_1 > 0$. Banks fund their loans with reservable (or insured) deposits, RD and with managed liabilities (or uninsured funds), ML. The marginal cost of reservable deposits and managed liabilities are: $r^D = d_0 + d_1 RD$ and $r^{ML} = u_0 + u_1 ML$ respectively. d_0 captures shocks to the supply of reservable deposits. It is assumed that $u_0 > d_0 > 0$ to capture the idea that federal deposit insurance is provided at subsidized rates.

Jayaratne and Morgan note that the key parameter in the model is u_1, which determines whether the marginal cost of external funds is flat or increasing. They assume that $d_1 > u_1 \geq 0$ indicating that the marginal cost of reservable deposits is steeper than the marginal cost of nonreservable funds. This assumption ensures that banks fund their marginal loans with uninsured funds. The evidence in this paper further suggests that it is flat: $u_1 = 0$.

In order to maximize profits, banks choose the optimal amount of loans and the cost minimizing levels of reservable deposits and managed liabilities. At the optimum level, the marginal revenue of loans equals the marginal cost of reservable deposits and managed liabilities: $r^L = r^{RD} = r^{ML}$. The balance sheet condition requires that $L = RD + ML$. These two conditions and the above equations determine the equilibrium quantities of reservable deposits, managed liabilities, and loans: RD^*, ML^* and L^* respectively.

$$RD^* = [u_1(l_0 - d_0) - l_1(d_0 - u_0)] / [u_1(d_1 + l_1) + l_1 d_1]$$

$$ML^* = [d_1(l_0 - u_0) - l_1(d_0 - u_0)] / [u_1(d_1 + l_1) + l_1 d_1]$$

$$L^* = (l_0 - d_0)/l_1 - d_1 [u_1(l_0 - d_0) - l_1(d_0 - u_0)] / [u_1(d_1 + l_1) + l_1 d_1]\}_1$$

The first result in Jayaratne and Morgan - indicates that "a reduction in the supply of deposits (that is an increase in d_0) will reduce bank lending if and only if the marginal cost of uninsured funds is increasing"(p.81). Formally:

$$\frac{\partial L^*}{\partial d_0} = \frac{-u_1}{u_1(d_1 + l_1) + l_1 d_1}$$

The empirical evidence in this paper, which suggests that $u_1 = 0$ implies that $\frac{\partial L^*}{\partial d_0} = 0$, that is, a reduction in the supply of reservable deposits leaves bank lending unchanged.

Under these circumstances, an increase in loan demand (say because more customers honor their loan commitments following a tightening) results in an increase in equilibrium bank loans. In other words, a positive shock to loan demand (that is an increase in l_0) increases the equilibrium quantity of loans:

$$\frac{\partial L^*}{\partial l_0} = \frac{l_1(u_1 + d_1)}{[(u_1 + d_1) + l_1 d_1]Y_1} = \frac{1}{1 + l_1} > 0 \text{ when } u_1 = 0.$$

Consequently, if contractionary monetary policy triggers an increase in loan demand, the money multiplier mechanism, which predicts a decline in loans or securities, fails.

Table 1: Granger Causality Tests (1990-2007)*

Variables are in log levels

	I. Required Reserves	II. Reservable Deposits	III. Bank Loans	IV. Total Balances	V. Managed Liabilities	VI. Large Time Deposits
1. Required Reserves		0.0000	0.5162	0.0000	0.5336	0.8551
2. Reservable Deposits	0.6015		0.3622	0.0000	0.3941	0.0190
3. Bank Loans	0.1868	0.0002		0.1494	0.0002	0.0001
4. Total Balances	0.0014	0.0053	0.8717		0.6177	0.2847
5. Managed Liabilities	0.4540	0.0140	0.7573	0.8350		0.0796
6. Large Time Deposits	0.3141	0.5679	0.0014	0.9917	0.6514	

Variables are in first differences

	I. Required Reserves	II. Reservable Deposits	III. Bank Loans	IV. Total Balances	V. Managed Liabilities	VI. Large Time Deposits
1. Required Reserves		0.0000	0.8042	0.0000	0.9277	0.0006
2. Reservable Deposits	0.6813		0.1725	0.0003	0.7637	0.4208
3. Bank Loans	0.3197	0.0198		0.2133	0.0006	0.0313
4. Total Balances	0.0124	0.2147	0.9867		0.7757	0.4337
5. Managed Liabilities	0.7086	0.1483	0.2753	0.7656		0.8400
6. Large Time Deposits	0.4243	0.0006	0.0731	0.0000	0.0935	

*The month that corresponds to September 11, 2001 is excluded from the sample.

For each forecasting variable, the entries across each row are the marginal significance levels for omitting six lags of the variable indicated in the column heading.

Analysis includes six lags of each variable.

Source: Authors' calculations.

Table 2: Variance Decomposition Analysis of Loans

Monthly Frequency

	VAR Specification: FFR, CPI, Loans, Reservable Deposits, Managed Liabilities, Securities, Unemployment		VAR Specification: FFR, CPI, Loans, Reservable Deposits, Large Time Deposits, Securities, Unemployment	
	Percentage of the Forecast Error in Bank Loans Explained by:		Percentage of the Forecast Error in Bank Loans Explained by:	
Period	Reservable Deposits	Managed Liabilities	Reservable Deposits	Large Time Deposits
1	0.00	0.00	0.00	0.00
2	0.08	0.10	0.67	0.96
3	0.37	0.27	1.35	2.60
4	1.97	2.06	2.45	3.21
5	4.20	3.35	3.94	3.66
6	5.14	5.25	4.43	5.02
7	5.54	5.79	4.70	7.04
8	5.66	6.20	4.94	9.47
9	5.50	6.42	4.82	11.93
10	5.35	6.43	4.57	14.63
11	5.45	6.25	4.28	17.58
12	5.55	6.06	3.96	20.45
13	5.56	5.86	3.61	23.07
14	5.53	5.66	3.27	25.45
15	5.42	5.44	2.98	27.51
16	5.27	5.20	2.73	29.26
17	5.09	4.99	2.53	30.71
18	4.88	4.79	2.38	31.92
19	4.66	4.61	2.27	32.91
20	4.45	4.43	2.20	33.71
21	4.24	4.28	2.16	34.38
22	4.05	4.13	2.13	34.92
23	3.87	3.99	2.13	35.34
24	3.70	3.86	2.14	35.67

Variables are ordered as they are listed in the VAR specifications in each column heading.

Source: Authors' calculations.

Table 3: Balance Sheets for Banks of Different Sizes

1994.Q1

	Below 75	75-90	90-95	95-98	98-99	over 99
Number of Banks	7787	1557	519	312	104	104
Mean Assets (1994 $ millions)	53.70	194.52	443.07	1232.90	4000.21	15137.65
Median Assets (1994 $ millions)	47.02	182.67	426.05	1079.11	3765.98	10299.89
Fraction of total assets	0.13	0.09	0.07	0.12	0.13	0.47
Fraction of total loans	0.12	0.09	0.07	0.12	0.13	0.47
Cash	0.05	0.05	0.05	0.06	0.07	0.09
Securities	0.35	0.33	0.30	0.27	0.26	0.19
Total loans	0.53	0.56	0.59	0.60	0.60	0.57
Total deposits	0.88	0.87	0.84	0.81	0.76	0.67
Transaction deposits	0.27	0.27	0.26	0.25	0.26	0.21
Large deposits	0.08	0.07	0.07	0.07	0.06	0.05
Brokered deposits	0.00	0.00	0.01	0.01	0.01	0.02
Subordinated debt	0.00	0.00	0.00	0.00	0.00	0.01
Other Liabilities	0.10	0.09	0.09	0.08	0.08	0.09
Equity	0.10	0.09	0.09	0.08	0.08	0.07

2007.Q2

	Below 75	75-90	90-95	95-98	98-99	over 99
Number of Banks	5046	1009	336	202	67	68
Mean Assets (2007 $ millions)	89.25	359.61	771.81	1786.65	4755.34	36908.83
Median Assets (2007 $ millions)	76.44	347.04	736.12	1648.24	4678.33	20541.57
Fraction of total assets	0.11	0.09	0.06	0.08	0.07	0.59
Fraction of total loans	0.11	0.09	0.07	0.09	0.07	0.56
Cash	0.04	0.03	0.03	0.03	0.04	0.05
Securities	0.21	0.18	0.18	0.17	0.21	0.17
Total loans	0.67	0.72	0.72	0.72	0.65	0.62
Total deposits	0.84	0.81	0.80	0.77	0.71	0.69
Transaction deposits	0.22	0.13	0.10	0.09	0.08	0.06
Large deposits	0.17	0.17	0.16	0.14	0.14	0.10
Brokered deposits	0.03	0.05	0.05	0.05	0.04	0.04
Subordinated debt	0.00	0.00	0.00	0.00	0.00	0.02
Other Liabilities	0.11	0.10	0.10	0.11	0.12	0.13
Equity	0.11	0.10	0.10	0.11	0.12	0.11

Source: Federal Reserve Bank of Chicago (http://www.chicagofed.org/banking_information/financial_institute_reports_des_call_main.cfm).

Table 4: Balance Sheets for Banks for Alternative Classifications

A. Composition of Bank Balance Sheets based on $\frac{\text{Securities}}{\text{Assets}}$ as of 2007.Q2

	Below 20	20-40	40-60	60-80	over 80
Number of Banks	1345	1346	1345	1346	1346
Mean Assets (2007 $ millions)	696.68	1054.78	537.37	568.51	309.86
Median Assets (2007 $ millions)	129.34	135.90	122.64	94.85	68.53
Fraction of total assets	0.22	0.33	0.17	0.18	0.10
Fraction of total loans	0.26	0.36	0.18	0.15	0.05
Cash	0.03	0.03	0.03	0.07	0.05
Securities	0.06	0.13	0.18	0.25	0.49
Total loans	0.76	0.70	0.71	0.54	0.35
Total deposits	0.68	0.73	0.76	0.74	0.76
Transaction deposits	0.08	0.08	0.09	0.09	0.12
Large deposits	0.13	0.10	0.14	0.12	0.12
Brokered deposits	0.09	0.03	0.03	0.02	0.01
Subordinated debt	0.02	0.01	0.01	0.01	0.00
Other Liabilities	0.16	0.12	0.11	0.11	0.09
Equity	0.14	0.10	0.10	0.10	0.08

B. Composition of Bank Balance Sheets based on $\frac{\text{Capital}}{\text{Assets}}$ as of 2007.Q2

	Below 20	20-40	40-60	60-80	over 80
Number of Banks	1345	1346	1345	1346	1346
Mean Assets (2007 $ millions)	851.62	769.10	538.58	377.82	630.19
Median Assets (2007 $ millions)	142.63	145.68	113.58	88.72	67.09
Fraction of total assets	0.27	0.24	0.17	0.12	0.20
Fraction of total loans	0.22	0.26	0.19	0.13	0.20
Cash	0.07	0.03	0.03	0.03	0.03
Securities	0.25	0.17	0.15	0.16	0.13
Total loans	0.53	0.69	0.74	0.72	0.65
Total deposits	0.74	0.75	0.75	0.77	0.64
Transaction deposits	0.09	0.08	0.09	0.11	0.08
Large deposits	0.12	0.10	0.14	0.14	0.12
Brokered deposits	0.03	0.03	0.04	0.03	0.07
Subordinated debt	0.01	0.01	0.01	0.01	0.01
Other Liabilities	0.09	0.10	0.11	0.12	0.20
Equity	0.07	0.09	0.10	0.12	0.19

Source: Federal Reserve Bank of Chicago
(http://www.chicagofed.org/banking_information/financial_institute_reports_des_call_main.cfm).

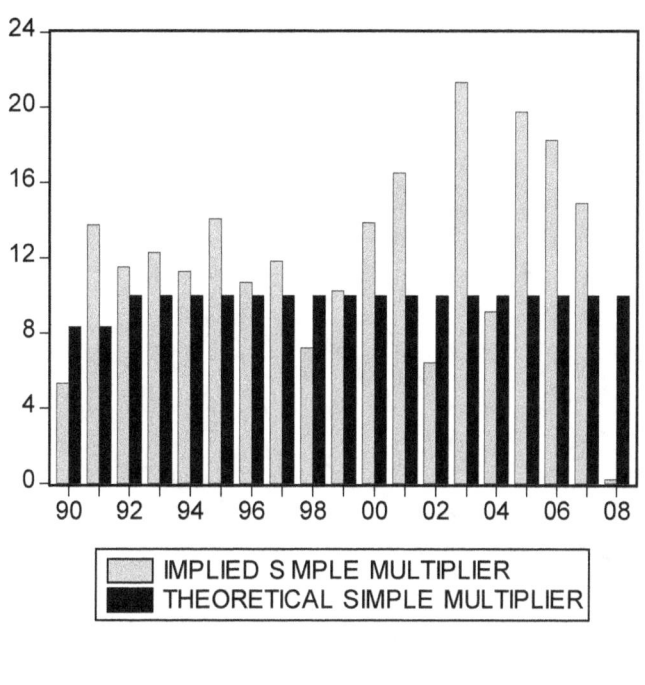

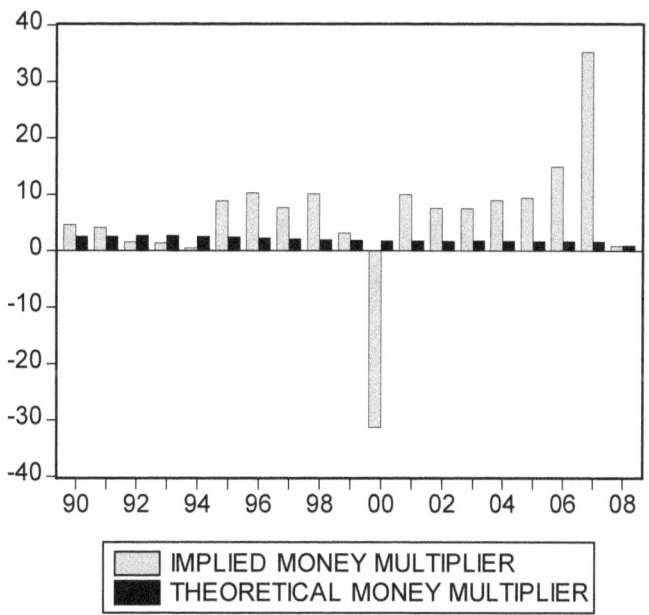

Figure 1: The Discrepancy between the Theoretical and the Actual Multiplier

Source: Simple multiplier: Federal Reserve Statistical Releases H.3 (Required reserves) and H.6 (reservable deposits); implied money multiplier: authors' calculations; theoretical money multiplier: Federal Reserve Statistical Releases H.3 (monetary base, excess reserves) and H.6 (reservable deposits, M2).

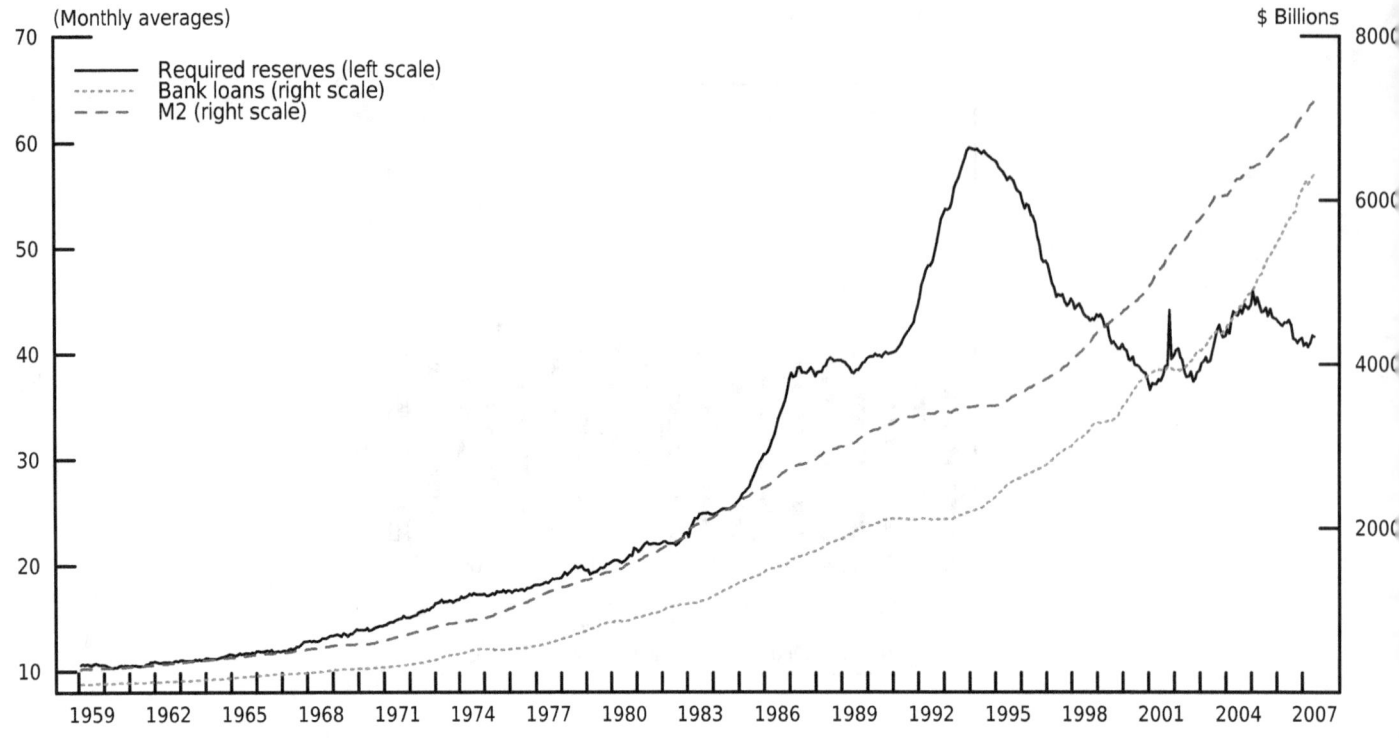

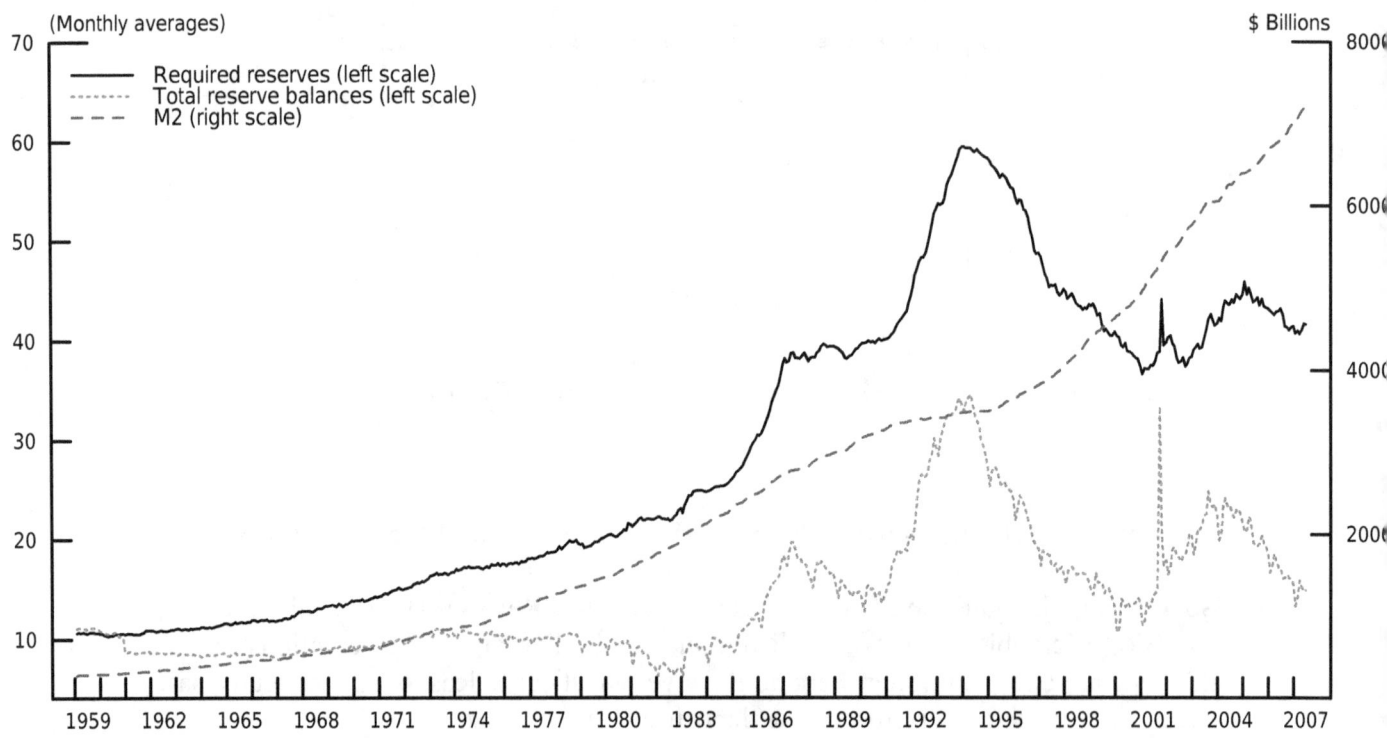

Figure 2: Monetary Aggregates and Bank Loans (1959-2007)

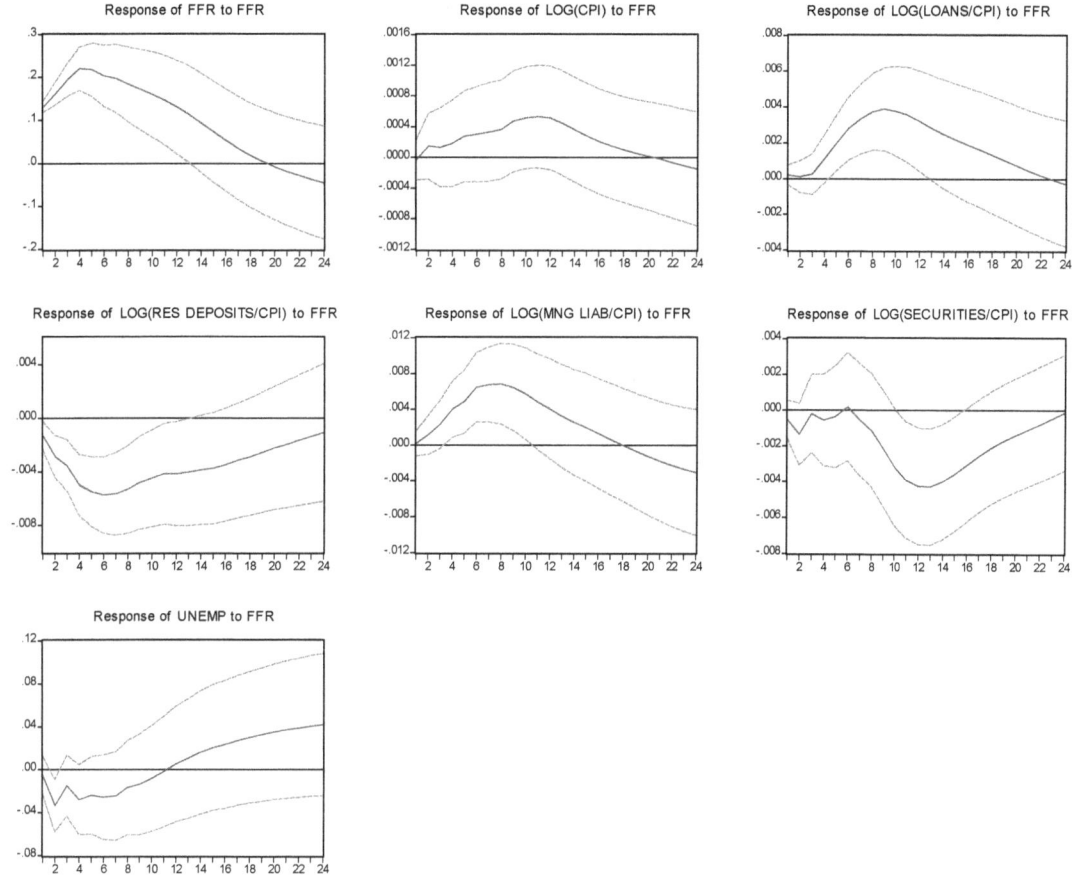

*excluding September 2001

where:

FFR:	Federal Funds Rate
CPI:	Consumer Price Index
Loans:	Total Bank Loans and Leases
Res Deposits:	Reservable Deposits
Mng Liab:	Managed Liabilities
Unemp:	Unemployment Rate

Figure 3: Bernanke and Blinder Updated (1990-2007)*

Source: Authors' calculations.

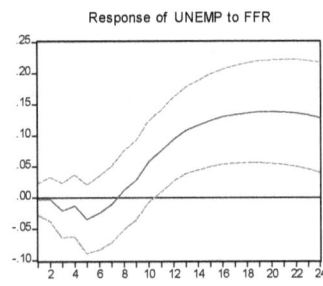

Figure 4: Bernanke and Blinder (1959-1978)

Source: Authors' calculations.

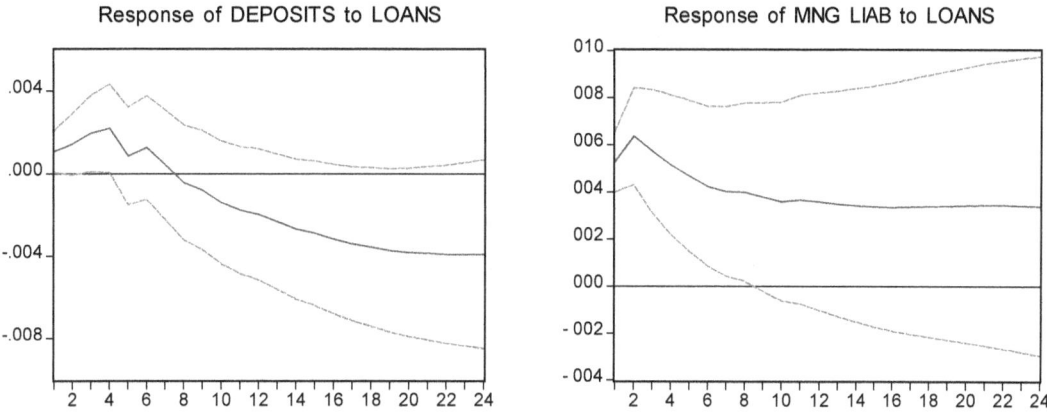

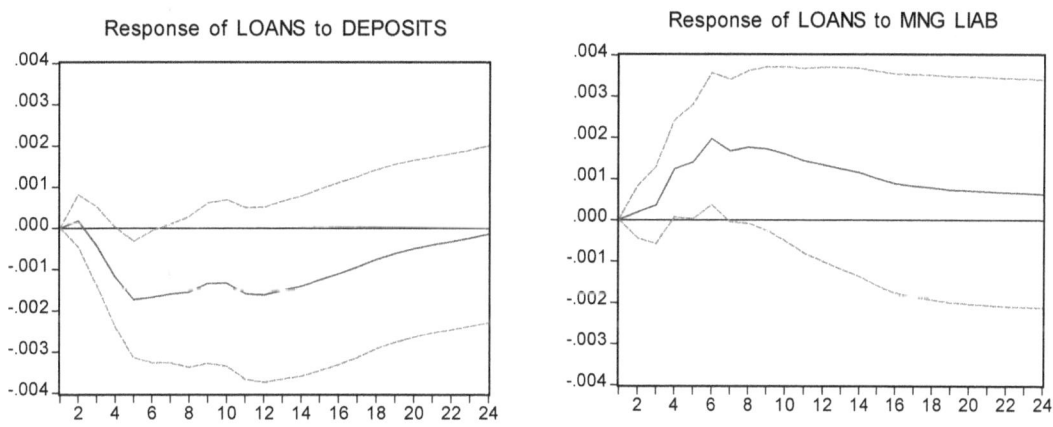

Figure 5: Bernanke and Blinder Updated (Cont'd)

Source: Authors' calculations.

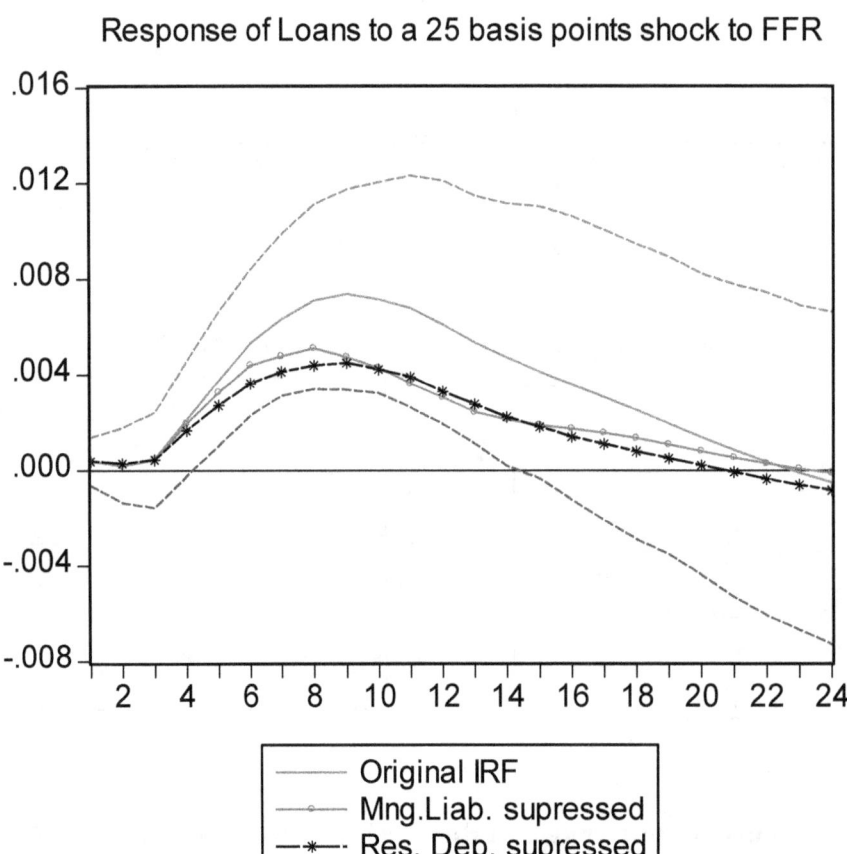

The dashed lines represent 95 percent confidence intervals computed by bootstrap method.

Figure 6: The Response of Bank Loans under Counterfactual Experiments

Source: Authors' calculations.

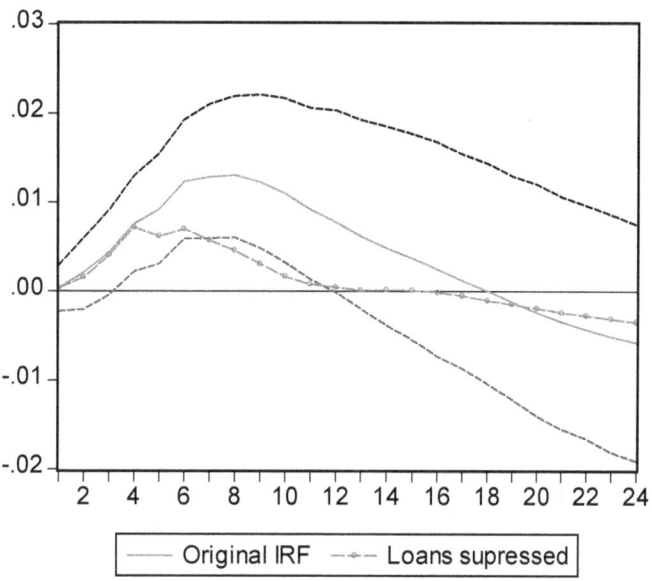

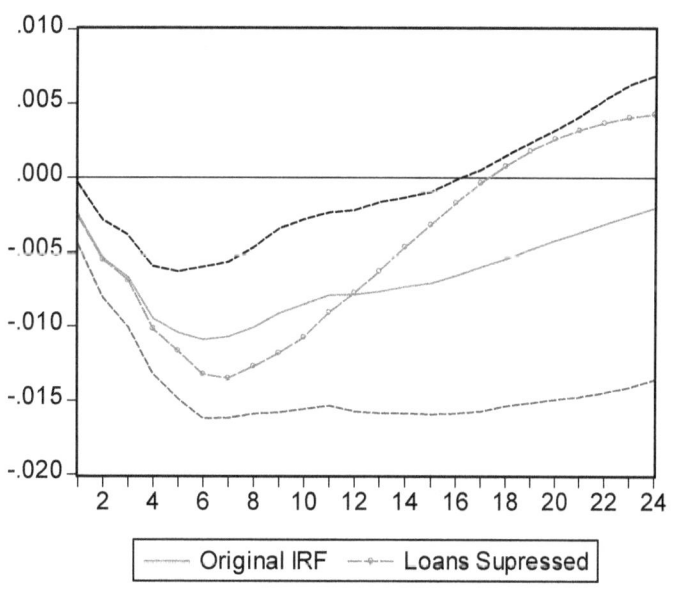

The dashed lines represent 95 percent confidence intervals computed by bootstrap method.

Figure 7: The Responses of Different Bank Liabilities under Counterfactual Experiments

Source: Authors' calculations.

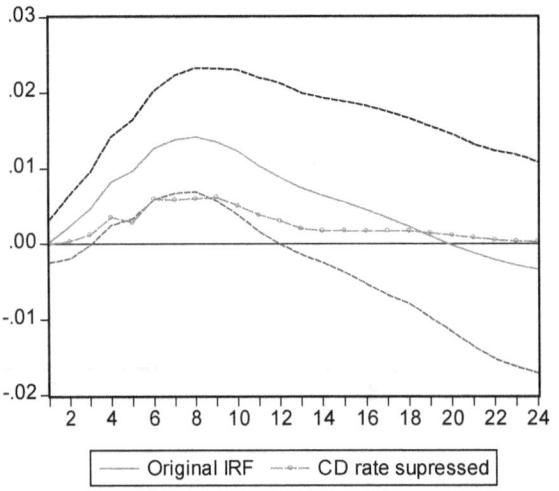

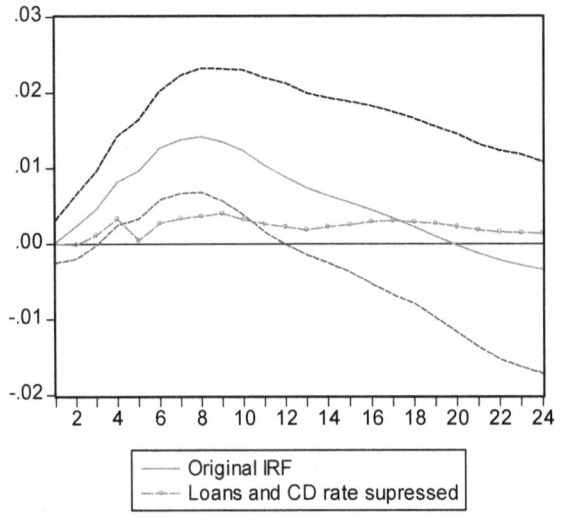

The dashed lines represent 95 percent confidence intervals computed by bootstrap method.

Figure 8: The Responses of Different Bank Liabilities under Counterfactual Experiments

Source: Authors' calculations.

Response to Funds Rate

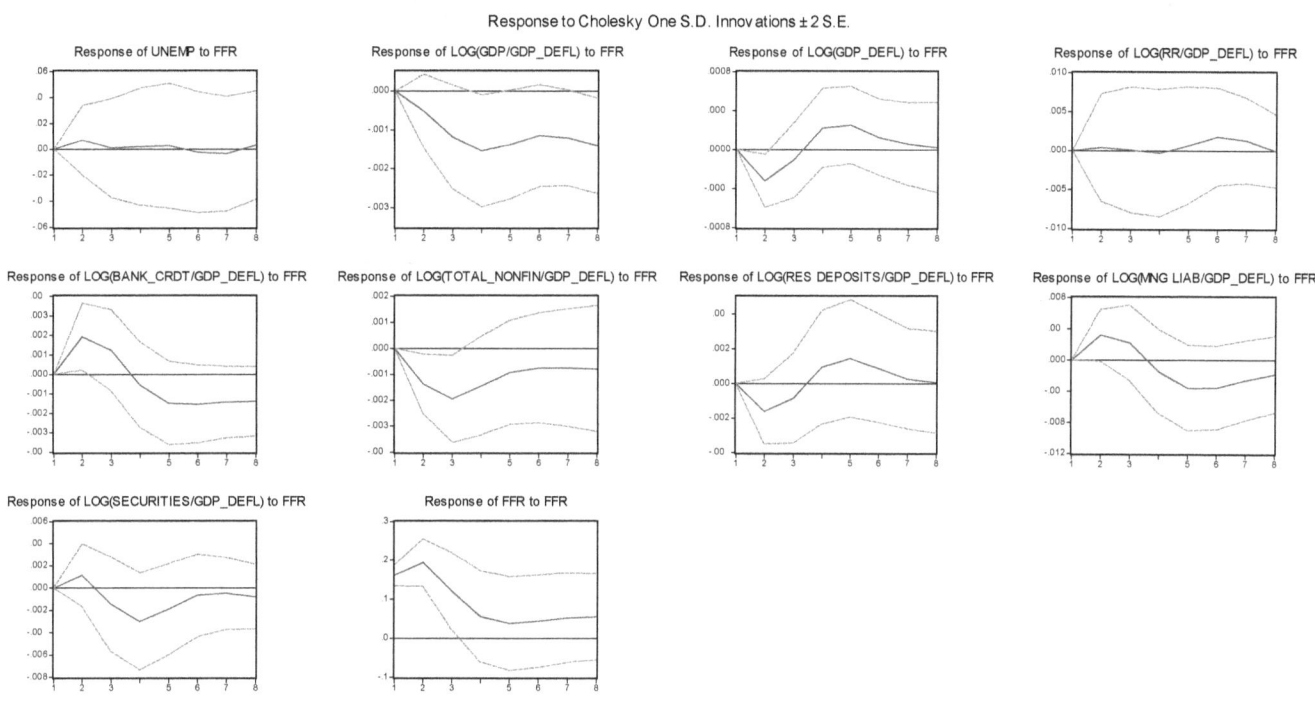

where:

FFR:	Federal Funds Rate
GDP_Defl:	GDP Deflator
Bank_Crdt:	Total Bank Loans
Total_nonfin:	Total Non-financial Borrowing
Re Deposits:	Reservable Deposits
Mng Liab:	Managed Liabilities
Unemp:	Unemployment Rate
RR:	Required Reserves

Figure 9: VAR Analysis at the Quarterly Frequency

Source: Authors' calculations.

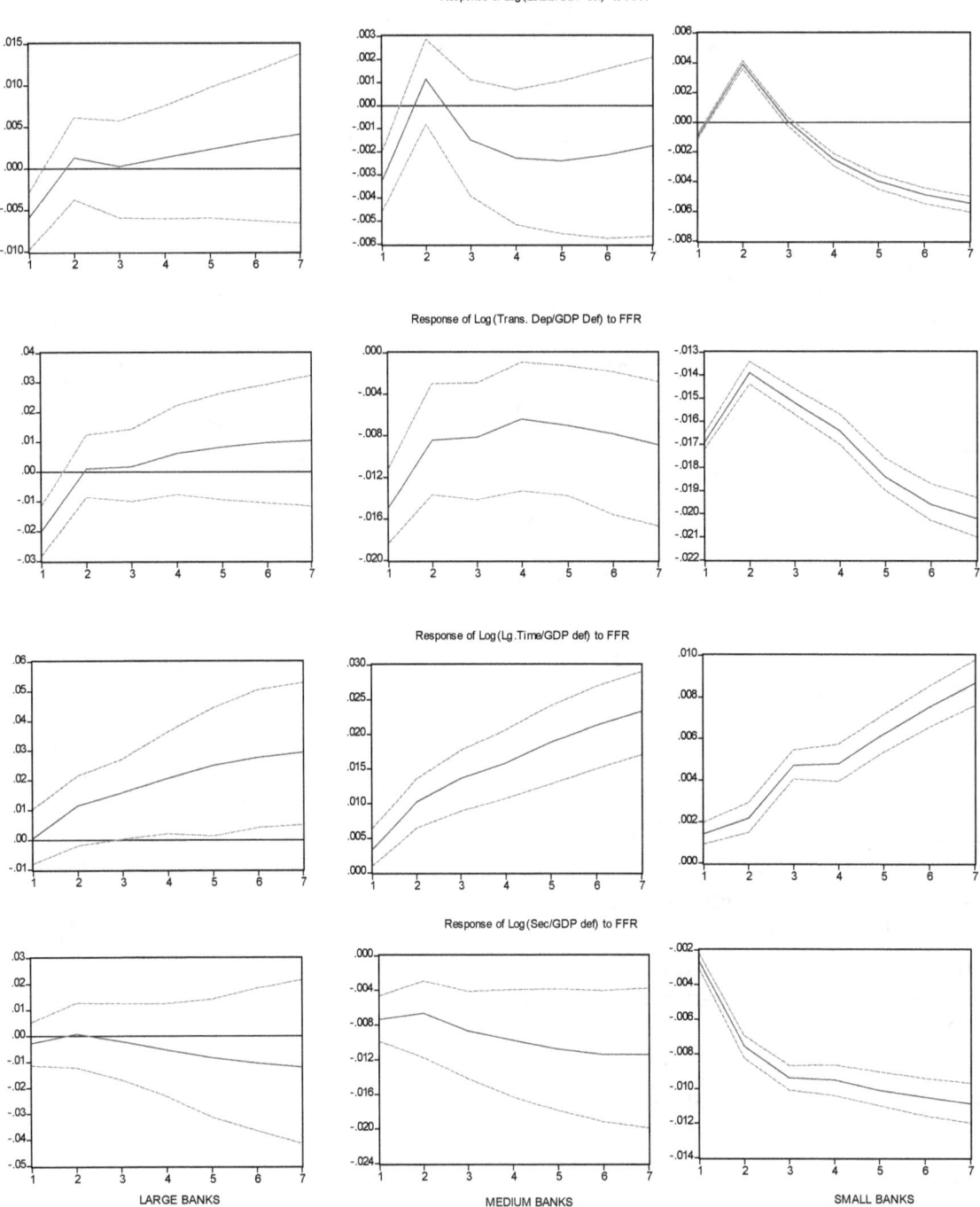

Figure 10: Panel VAR Analysis (Breakdown with respect to Asset Size)

Source: Authors' calculations.

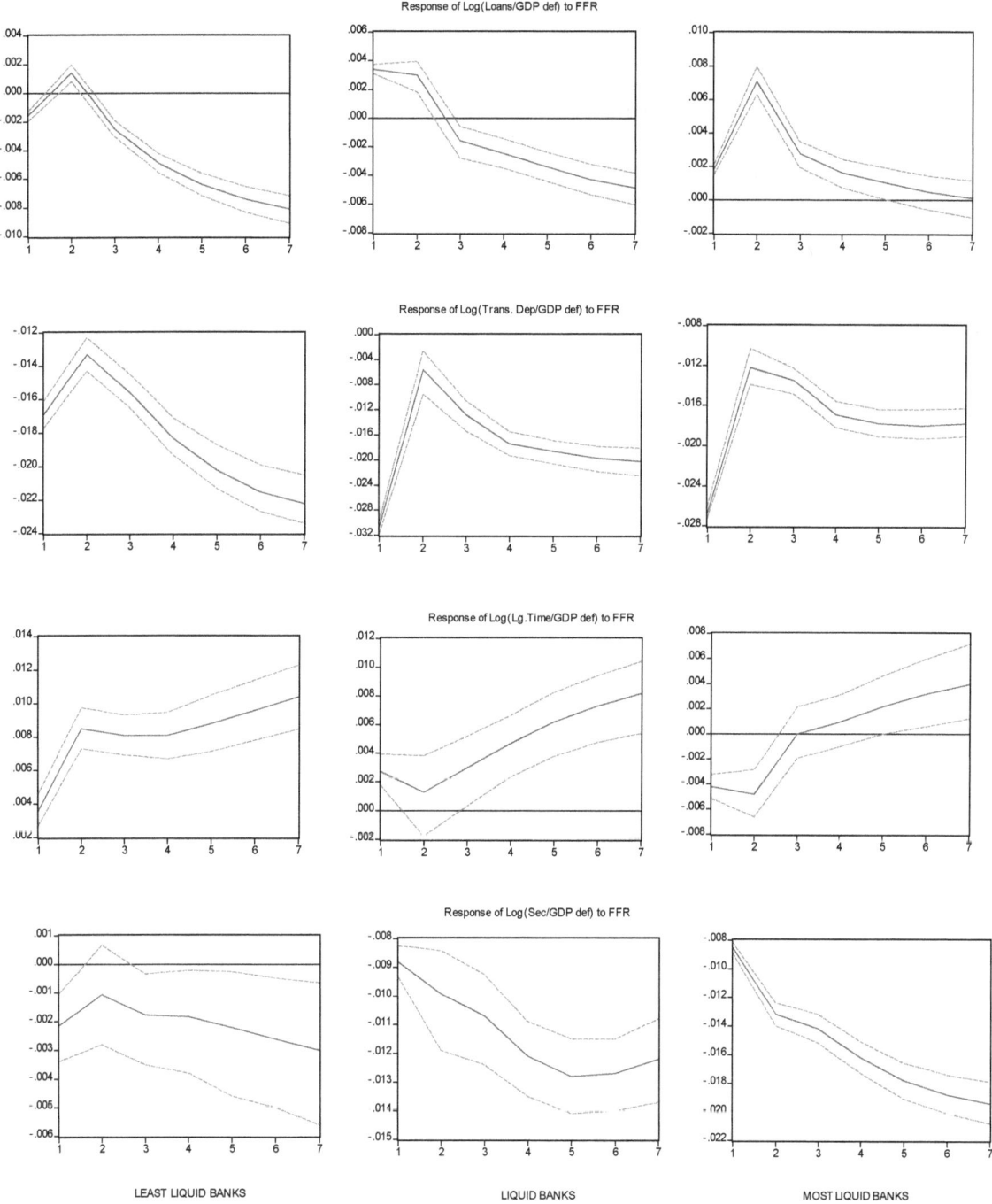

Figure 11a: Panel VAR Analysis (Breakdown with respect to $\frac{\text{Securities}}{\text{Assets}}$ Ratio)

Source: Authors' calculations.

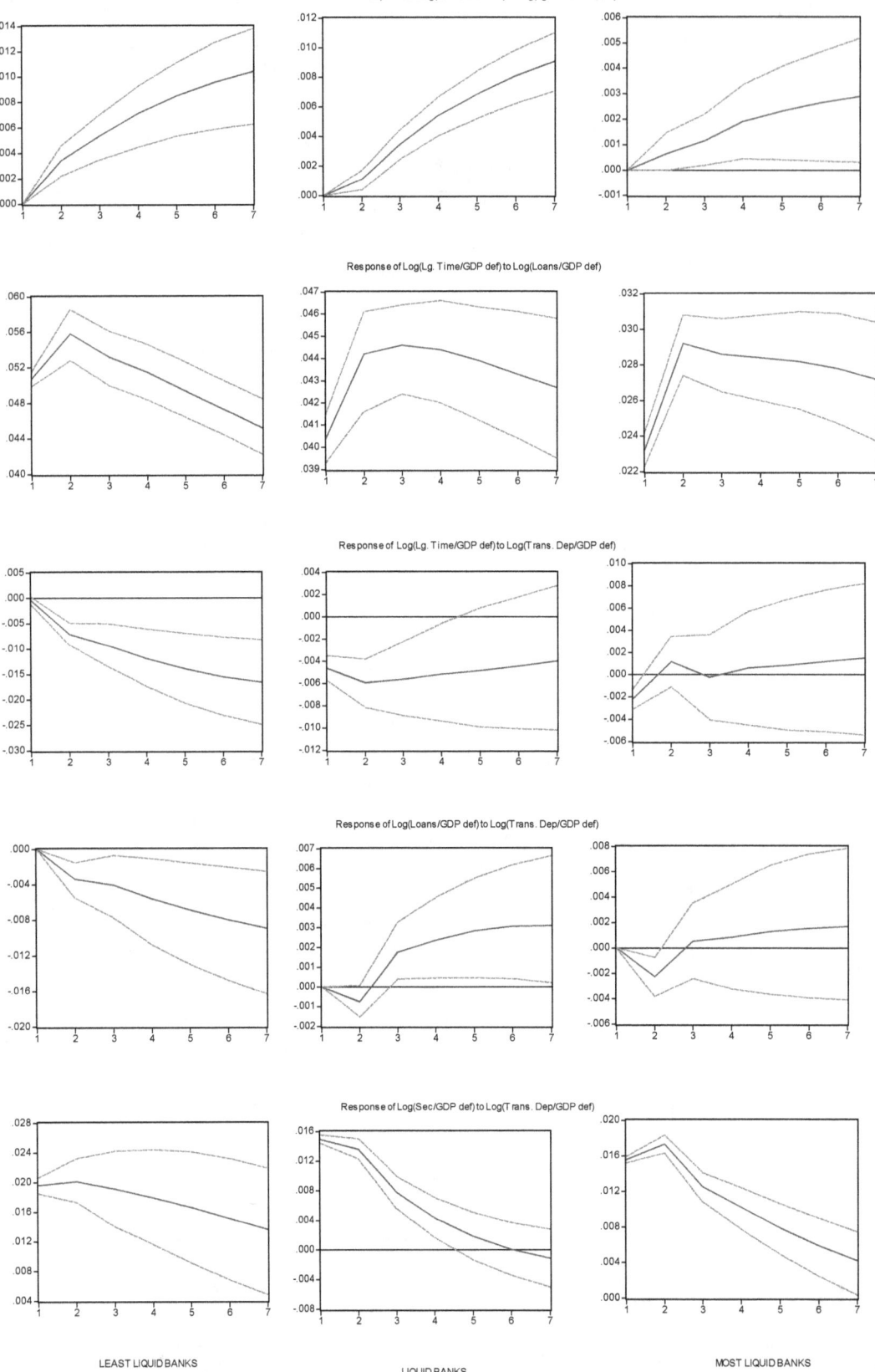

Figure 11b: Panel VAR Analysis (Breakdown with respect to $\frac{\text{Securities}}{\text{Assets}}$ Ratio)

Source: Authors' calculations.

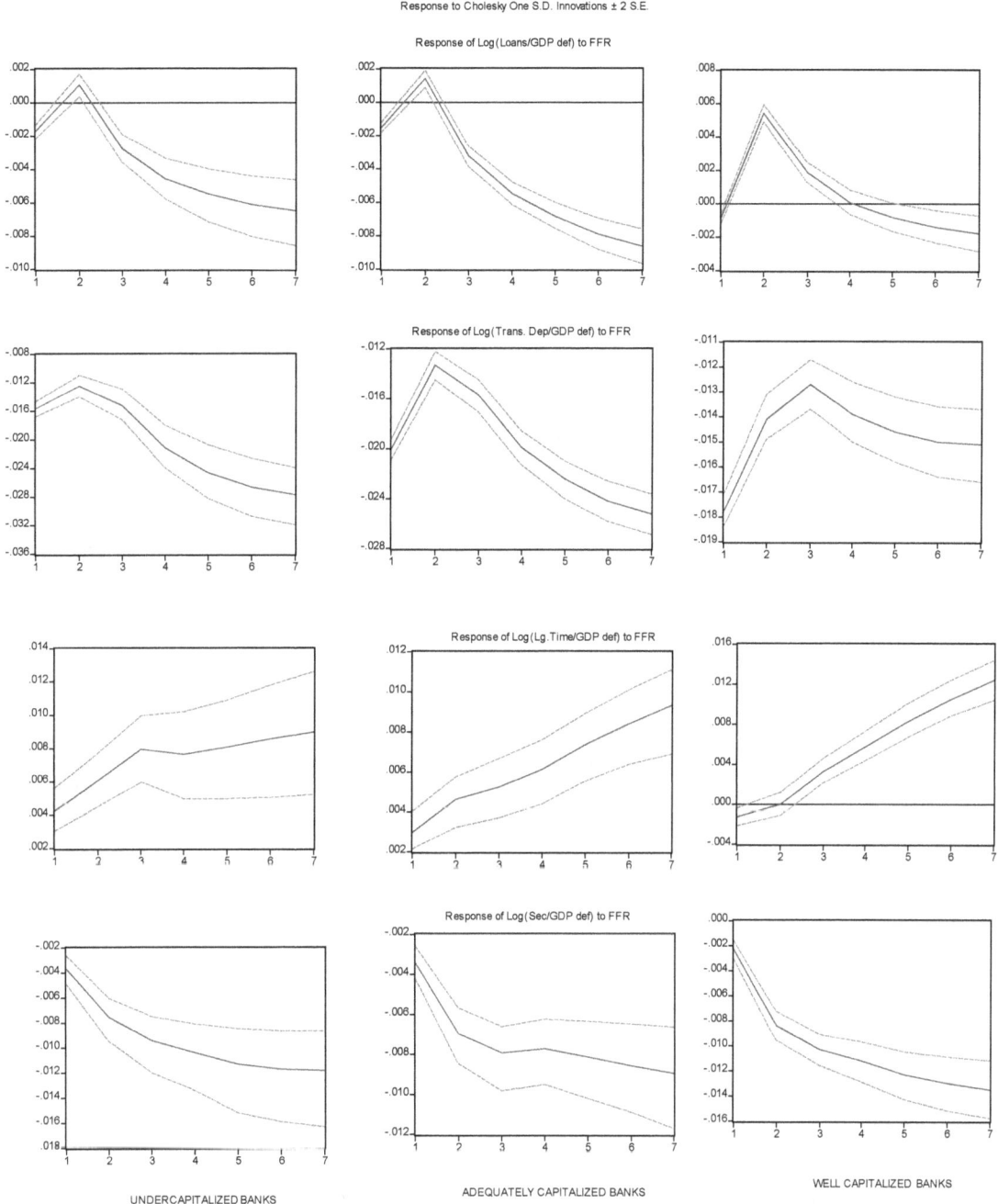

Figure 12: Panel VAR Analysis (Breakdown with respect to $\frac{\text{Capital}}{\text{Assets}}$ Ratio)

Source: Authors' calculations.

www.ingramcontent.com/pod-product-compliance
Lightning Source LLC
Chambersburg PA
CBHW081904170526
45167CB00007B/3137